A LINCOLNSHIRE CHILDHOOD

Helen Smethurst with her daughters: Honor, left, Pip, the baby, and Bunty, the author, on the right

A LINCOLNSHIRE CHILDHOOD

Ursula Brighouse

Illustrated by Henry Brighouse

ALAN SUTTON

First published in the United Kingdom in 1992
Alan Sutton Publishing Ltd · Phoenix Mill · Far Thrupp · Stroud
Gloucestershire

First published in the United States of America in 1992
Alan Sutton Publishing Inc · Wolfeboro Falls · NH 03896-0848

British Library Cataloguing in Publication Data

Brighouse, Ursula W.
Lincolnshire Childhood
I. Title
942.53083092

ISBN 0-7509-0251-5

Library of Congress Cataloging in Publication Data applied for

Typeset in 12/13pt Garamond.
Typesetting and origination by
Alan Sutton Publishing Limited.
Printed in Great Britain by
The Bath Press, Bath, Avon.

Contents

Foreword

'Grannie, tell us what it was like in the olden days' nagged my six grandchildren gently but persistently. It made me feel old – no, not so much old as *venerable*. I was the guardian of ancient truths, of the secrets of an age that had gone and they would never know unless I told them. I began to search in the deep cupboards of my mind where memories are stored and there I found all sorts of bits and pieces – like the contents of a junk-shop. Glimpses of life in the big house with servants, nannies and governesses: the closely knit village community with its joys and sorrows, its gossip, humour and, above all, its grittiness: the world of the shire horse and the singing ploughboy: an ancient landscape which man had shaped for himself over thousands of years and of the lavish gifts of nature that still formed part of it. Perhaps these things should be written down before I shuffle off this mortal coil and take my memories with me.

This book is in no true sense an autobiography. No attempt has been made to verify any of the tales contained herein, no research undertaken. They are told just as I remember them or, in some cases, heard them from others, and the memory, being notoriously fickle, may well have made a few adjustments for which I do not feel entirely responsible. The original idea was that the book should be written in collaboration with my sister Pip who so intimately shared the nursery of my young life. But we were both surprised to find how our memories differed. She recalled things I did not and vice versa. Even our joint memories varied as to time, place, names. Who is to know which of us was right? Now Pip has gone and there is only my word for what is written here.

The 1920s covered our young lives, giving us our standards and fashioning our concept of normality. It came as a shock to realize that for our parents' generation, which had survived the griefs and traumas of the Great War, nothing would ever be normal again. Some people shook their heads sadly and were too disillusioned to find good in anything. The young tended to go in the opposite direction, being wildly, superficially gay, the girls shortening their skirts, dancing the Charleston and trying to find husbands among a greatly depleted stock of eligible young men. But for the majority it was a matter of getting on with life, making the best of it and realizing slowly that this was it. There was no going back.

In October 1927 my childhood came to an abrupt end when I suffered a severe bout of polio. From being a running, jumping, tree-climbing child of ten I had to learn to lead a sedentary life. At first it never occurred to me that things would not be 'back to normal' next week, but when the final realization came it no longer mattered. A new life had opened up, a life of ideas and books, of music and art, of writing and handicrafts. Like those who survived the Great War, I discovered the adaptability of the human body and the resilience of the spirit. It was not, after all, the end of a Lincolnshire childhood – more the beginning of something else.

Ursula Brighouse
1992

Family

Family

Funny how some things stick in the mind – unimportant, insignificant things – while others of obvious importance, which might be expected to lodge in the filing system for ever, can be lost without trace.

I was fifteen months old on Armistice Day 1918 and, so the story went, I stood on the bars of the garden gate in High Wykeham, waving a small Union Jack and shouting 'Hullay, Hullay!' at the top of my voice. The air must have been almost unbearably charged with emotion – joy, excitement and overwhelming relief – and one would not have had to understand the meaning of it to experience the feeling. But no, all gone! Yet two months later and I have an indelible recollection of my father in army uniform, of being carried by him through the snow and of the smell of his Sam Browne belt. And still, after all these years, a certain smell of leather will trigger an immediate recall of that insignificant little scene, my father in his uniform, my seven-year-old sister Honor in a brown coat with a fur collar and fur cap, the snow – everything just as it was. Somewhere the mind retains a vivid picture which only requires a certain smell to bring it back again as if it were new.

My father never experienced the hell of the trenches in France, though he had a personal hell of his own to endure. He had been in the Territorial Army since 1898 and by 1915 he was a major in the Royal Artillery stationed near Cambridge, prior to being drafted to France with his battalion. He was a fine horseman and enjoyed nothing better than the chance army life offered to ride over open country. One winter's day he was jumping a hedge and ditch when his horse caught its foot in barbed wire, causing horse and rider to fall heavily into the ditch. His aide, who had been shutting a gate and was some way behind him, returned to camp to find no sign of the major. A search party was sent out to retrace the route and there they found him, trapped underneath the horse which was badly injured and had been writhing in agony for half an hour. The horse had to be shot before it could be dragged from the ditch and no one expected to find my father alive. He was badly crushed about the head and chest, unconscious, bleeding from the ears and totally unrecognizable.

The search party unhinged a nearby gate, lifted him on to it and carried him back to camp. Someone brought the news to my mother, who was billeted close by, and she came at once, just as she was – no time to grab a coat as she ran – and accompanied my father in the back of an open truck, which served as an ambulance, to the Military Hospital in Cambridge. During the journey she took off her cardigan and tried to cover him with it while she cradled his head in her lap to lessen the jolting. She was not aware of the bitter cold.

At the hospital my mother was told that although the major was still alive he could not survive the next hour. The fractures to his skull, spine, ribs and collar-bone were so severe that nothing could be done. All day she stayed by his bedside; night fell and he was still alive. But, said the doctors, he could not be expected to pull through the small hours. Morning came and he was still alive – no change in his condition but *still alive*. That night, after thirty-six hours without rest, my mother was taken home and told to try to get some sleep. They would contact her if there was any change.

Sleep indeed! Some hope! After a restless night my mother arose as soon as it was light and started to busy herself in the kitchen. Then, quite suddenly, a very remarkable thing happened. The kitchen was filled with a dazzling white light which seemed to envelop her and a voice somewhere within the brightness said, '*He's going to be all right.*'

The doctors at the hospital were somewhat taken aback by my mother's cheerful optimism. It was obvious that they had failed to get across to her the hopelessness of her husband's case. Gently but firmly they tried to spell it out in full, there was *nothing* they could do for him. She listened patiently, feeling almost sorry for them because *they* did not know what she knew. 'No, you don't understand. *He's going to be all right*,' she repeated doggedly, and they could not shake her.

Hullay! Hullay!

Hours grew into days, into weeks and my father regained consciousness. At first he was terribly disfigured by facial paralysis and by the way broken bones mend when they have not been set. And he had to contend with much pain and with loss of memory. But against all the odds he survived and his fight for life staggered the doctors and delighted my mother. Slowly but surely he recovered, his memory returned and his paralysed face began to resume its normal shape – though for many years he was subject to periodic headaches of devastating severity. At those times one eye would close and his mouth would start to drag round the corner towards his ear. I remember very clearly such bouts when Mummy would say 'Shh! Daddy's got a headache,' and the house was very silent, everyone on tiptoe.

Within eight months he was able to return to his duties, though these were now hedged about with restrictions. As part of his brain was no longer protected by bone he must not fire a gun, nor be in close proximity to guns being fired – a fine thing to impose on an artilleryman! Nor, to his great distress, was he allowed to ride a horse, though they gave him a motorbike and side-car which were probably more hazardous, both to himself and others.

And so the war years passed, my father training other men for the battles he would never have to fight himself – a fact that made him uneasy, not least when he was awarded the OBE for quelling a mutiny single-handed, for in certain quarters the OBE was contemptuously held to stand for 'Own Boys Exempt'. But he need not have worried. He was a natural leader of men, brave, determined, fair minded and resourceful, a man of great charisma and generosity of spirit. People would give him of their best and follow him to the ends of the earth.

Needless to say, these stories of wartime came from my mother. My father never mentioned any of the unpleasant things, although he sometimes referred to the reckless treasure-hunts with motorbike and side-car and the troop concerts in which he and my mother used to act and sing. 'I don't know how we dared,' he would add; he always hated making a fool of himself.

When it came to stories of his youth, before the war, he was a little more forthcoming and in response to our clamouring, 'Daddy, tell us about the time you escaped out of the window', he would embark on a strange tale of local history in which he had played a part. What the truth of it was I do not know, but as I remember him telling us, snuggled round the drawing-room fire on a winter's evening, it went like this.

My father, William, was the son of Henry Smethurst, a Grimsby trawler owner. In 1901 there was a catastrophic strike of trawlermen that brought the port to a halt. It lasted several months and was particularly hard on the deckhands, many of them young married men with families, who received no strike pay and no dole. If it had not been for charity and soup kitchens people might well have starved to death. My father, a hot-blooded twenty-year-old incensed at the hardship, took it into his head that the strike must be broken by getting a trawler to sea. As the lock-keepers had come out in support of the seamen, any scheme would involve not only finding a volunteer crew willing to run the gauntlet of the strikers, who were in an ugly mood, but also of managing to open the lock gates at high tide.

The plan was carefully laid and very nearly succeeded. My father was in the dock offices waiting for news that the trawler was safely out to sea when word got around among the strikers of what was happening. A huge crowd of furious men, armed with anything they could lay their hands on, converged on the offices where they forced the door and proceeded to wreck the place.

My father had to escape through an upstairs window at the back of the building and clambered down some roofs into an alley and ran for his life, pursued by the angry mob. The police finally managed to hold them at the railway crossing and, after a dramatic and official reading of the Riot Act by the chief magistrate, the trouble subsided and within a few days the strike collapsed.

My parents married in 1911 and my mother found the task of settling down in my father's world very difficult, but she accomplished it with good grace and without complaint. The life-styles of the two families were extraordinarily different. My mother's family were Lakelanders, her father a talented but struggling horticulturist and landscape architect. They were a highly artistic and happy-go-lucky family with an ever-open door for artists, writers, musicians, thinkers and a steady stream of promising youngsters. Grandpa was deeply influenced by William Morris and the Arts and Crafts Movement, and was a devoted disciple of Ruskin. My mother trained as a sculptress and silversmith at the Storey Institute in Lancaster and knew a good deal about architectural styles and the history of art. She was just as

Trawlers in Grimsby Docks

likely to spend the morning creating something of beauty or making music with friends as making the beds and dusting the dining-room – a tendency which rather shocked my father.

His family had come to Grimsby two generations earlier, in the wake of the railway line and the deep dock at Grimsby. These had created a boom town and from the 1850s up to the First World War sizeable fortunes were made in the fishing industry. My great-grandfather may or may not have heard of Ruskin but he did have a deeply ingrained social conscience entirely compatible with his Nonconformist and Teetotal background. He gave lavishly of his time, energy and wealth to building schools and to improving the pay and working conditions of fishermen, and was also active in local government, being Mayor of Grimsby twice. His son, also Henry (my grandfather), followed in his footsteps and was alderman for fifty years. But Grannie would not let him be mayor because she said they did not have the money to do the job in style. As so often happens to people in this situation, my grandparents found their respectability in sticking rigidly to the narrow rules of society. The cultural highlight of their year was the annual rendering of Handel's *Messiah* at the chapel, and their general moral rectitude encouraged a certain censoriousness. One did not just drop in unexpectedly at 6, Pelham Terrace; one visited in one's carriage at the conventional hour and left the appropriate calling cards. 'Large frogs in little puddles' my mother might have been tempted to say, and, indeed, the family did not greatly approve of my mother who, they felt, didn't know how to behave properly. She used to endure frequent humiliations at their hands and recalled an occasion when, as a shy young bride, she was pressed to sing a song for the family's entertainment. Horrified at the idea, she at first refused but they kept pressing her until finally she sat down at the grand piano and accompanied herself in a popular song called 'Tommy Lad'. It was greeted with total silence.

My mother would have found life intolerable but for the fact that she managed to find it all extremely funny. It was her light touch and quiet sense of the ridiculous that most endeared her to my father. She used to tell us a tale that illustrated the point nicely. On our bureau stood a tiny silver cup which my mother had won at the Ladies Rifle Club, being the Champion Shot for 1913. The members were told that the trophies, to be presented later, could be seen in the window of Palethorpes the jewellers. And there in the window was a very handsome silver trophy, nearly 2 feet high, towering over and almost totally obscuring a few smaller cups and medals. My mother reported excitedly to my father, adding, 'But I can't walk through the streets carrying that great thing.' So a taxi was ordered. The great day arrived and my mother was presented with her cup, all of four inches high, which she carried the three hundred yards home in the taxi. Once safely behind their own front door the two of them nearly died laughing. Had the error been my father's, his natural reaction would have been anger and embarrassment, from which my mother's humour would unerringly save him.

Settling Down

Settling Down

The war ended in November 1918 and my father was demobbed in the new year of 1919. That meant returning to Lincolnshire and the job which was waiting for him in the family firm. The war had not been kind to the business. Trawlers had been commandeered by the Royal Navy for use as mine-sweepers, and Icelandic trawlers had managed to capture a large part of the fishing. For many there was no way back and the future looked bleak. It fell to my father to drag his reluctant family into pastures new, selling the ageing trawlers for scrap metal at heart-breaking prices and launching boldly into a future in processing fish caught by others. There was much opposition but his move paid off in the end.

My mother dreaded the thought of returning to that stifling little world, with its social round, business talk and emphasis on money. It was hardly surprising that visits to Pelham Terrace were infrequent and dutiful, and as a result I do not remember my Smethurst grandparents very well. Grandpa was a dapper little man, rather bald and with a white moustache – a man of few words and less humour, but a prodigiously hard worker. The story was told that if his carriage was held up by a train at the level-crossing on his way to work in the morning, he would get out, cross the line and continue walking until his carriage caught up with him – so as not to waste time.

Grannie was a good-looking woman of considerable presence. I can see her now, with the sunlight falling on her pretty white hair as she sat by the big window, working away at an enormous jig-saw puzzle on a special baize-topped table. The pieces were wooden and not interlocking and there was no picture on the box lid for guidance. A large puzzle would take several weeks to complete. I was always anxious to 'help' and Grannie would show me how to look for the straight-edged border pieces first.

But one day I blotted my copy-book and the sharp recollection of it has stayed with me, as such things are apt to do. On this occasion a lovely box of chocolates was handed round. We rarely had chocolates at home and, oh, it was such a delicious treat. The open box was then left temptingly on the table. After a while I could bear it no longer and asked if I might have another.

'Helen,' Grannie boomed in her best Lady Bracknell voice, 'has this child *no* manners?'

My mother hung her head and said, 'I'm very sorry, Grannie. It won't happen again.' Nothing was said to me directly, but I was uncomfortably aware that I had caused my mother acute embarrassment.

So it was for the sake of my mother's happiness that house-hunting took place at a long arm's-length from Grimsby. For the time being we were able to live in Grannie's summer cottage in the country. It was in the middle of a pretty Wold village, the house built of brick turned brown with age. It had a steep gabled roof and sash windows opening almost down to the ground, so that I could run in and out. In front of the cottage was an old, spreading cherry tree and at the far end of the garden, by the potting shed and the water butt, stood a mulberry tree around whose trunk were propped lengths of wood – firewood and bean sticks – till it resembled an Indian wigwam. A good hiding place! Over the garden wall and across the village street was a large round duck-pond which in days gone by had provided the inhabitants with drinking water – and a good many water-borne parasites and diseases, no doubt.

The beauties of the North Lincolnshire countryside are by no means obvious. The area cannot boast the attractions of Kent's 'garden of England' nor the stone villages of the Cotswolds; it cannot lay claim to Devon redland hills nor the trees of Constable Country. Its charm comes to one slowly and subtly and water-colour artists have long appreciated its wide, four-fifths skies and the patchwork of fields rolling away to the distant line of the Humber or Wolds. During that early summer of 1919 there were many expeditions of discovery. I well remember the excitement of mustard fields in full bloom, so brilliant a yellow that they could be seen for miles, the white froth of cow parsley along the hedgerows, the heady fragrance of bean fields in flower and the coveys of young partridges that often scurried along the road in front of the car.

My father bought Thornton Hall and there we moved in September 1919. I remember nothing of the move itself, though I was aware of a certain unease and uncertainty. At Grannie's cottage, although there were servants, the smallness of the house threw us together as a family so that one always knew where everybody was. There was a cosy intimacy about the cottage which felt both warm and secure. Thornton, on the other hand, was a Queen Anne mansion of some seventeen bedrooms. Outside it was classical and imposing, with fine stone pediments to the windows of the central block and two lower wings or pavilions, one either side, which gave a pleasing proportion to the whole pile. Inside there were long passages and flights of stairs, and though the main rooms were high and elegantly panelled, they were also extremely draughty. And the house was isolated from the village. Never again would I stand on the bars of the gate and say hello to people walking by.

Thornton Hall

At the exact time the move was being made my mother disappeared from the scene and was nowhere to be found. The reason for her absence soon became apparent. She had gone into a nursing home in York to give birth to my younger sister Pip. And three weeks later home they came. I remember Pip's arrival very clearly. She was brought up to the nursery for me to inspect, wrapped copiously in a shawl and in layers of clothing at least a yard long, carried by Nanny who was as excited as though she'd won the Derby and accompanied by Mummy who tried to fob me off with a doll. 'No,' I said firmly, 'I want the *real* one!' There was no feeling of jealousy – I rather liked the newcomer even though she wasn't much use. Her presence added a good deal of life and interest to the nursery. Mummy never made any secret of the fact that she did not much like young children and she took very little interest in either of us younger ones. This partly accounted for the lack of jealousy I felt for Pip, but the main reason, I suspect, was due to a happy division of honours in the nursery whereby Pip was the sole property of Nanny while I was blissful in the hands of the nursery maid – the one and only adorable Minnie Hank.

Side-splitting entertainment with Minnie Hank

I suppose Minnie Hank was not more than fifteen years of age and certainly not more than 4 ft 10 in high. She had a wren-like quality about her, lack of stature being more than compensated for by a perky and highly comical nature. Afternoon walks were always fun. While Nanny (bonnet perched on her head and tied under her chin with a stiff bow) sedately pushed Pip in the high, grey, coach-built pram – large wheels at the back, smaller ones in front – I was in the push-chair enjoying all sorts of side-splitting entertainment as Minnie galloped and turned in tight manoeuvres and pretended to die of exhaustion. The push-chair was a weird and unique vehicle made of wood painted green with designs and scrolls on the side panels, the foot end of it curled up like a Russian horse-drawn sleigh. By kicking it vigorously with strong shoes one could make a really good noise.

Minnie had many gifts, one of which was the making of soft toys. A beloved legacy of her time with us was a monkey made of brown velvet, with yellow shammy-leather face, ears, hands and feet, and two brown boot buttons for eyes, peering out from slits in the face to give it a bemused and sleepy expression. The monkey was, of course, called Minnie Hank and was a prized member of our 'family' until we grew up and finally put childish things behind us.

Minnie Hank stayed for about two years and after she left we soon lost touch. It was therefore a matter of great excitement when in 1945 we suddenly read in our newspapers that Minnie Hank had been awarded a medal for the most extraordinary gallantry. She had been nanny to an army family in the Far East when she found herself and the five children in her charge (including a baby) cut off behind enemy lines by a sudden Japanese advance. Minnie made five separate journeys by night, smuggling the children one by one through the Japanese lines to be safely reunited with their family. *Our* Minnie Hank! Just fancy that!

Although Mummy seemed vague and aloof from our nursery life for much of the time she could be surprisingly swift and decisive when the occasion demanded. I vividly recall one such occasion. When Nanny and Minnie Hank left us there followed a brief reign of terror under Miss Reynolds, who brought great misery to the nursery. I was always in trouble and seemed to spend my life in the corner.

One day Miss Reynolds, beside herself with fury over my recalcitrant behaviour (I had stamped on her foot), lifted me up and sat me on the toy shelf – first removing the toys out of my reach. The shelf was long and narrow and about 5 feet from the floor. I was told that if I moved I would fall off, which was very probably true. Actually, the shelf was preferable to the corner because at least I could see what was going on and I had no fear of heights. But I had not been there very long before Mummy paid one of her rare visits to the nursery.

She summed the situation up in a split second. In two quick strides she had reached me and I was in her arms. There was a short exchange of words and Miss Reynolds left the room. Within an hour we watched from the nursery window as her luggage was loaded into the car and George drove her away to the station. We never saw her again. The incident was strangely reassuring.

Then Mary came and a wonderful serenity settled on the nursery. I remember no punishments but a quiet, gentle presence and although Mary, too, found me recalcitrant, she had her own way of dealing with it. I dearly loved to get my own way and when I could not my reaction might be a flaming temper and a running kick at the furniture (the old upright piano was the most satisfactory thing to kick because it answered back), or, more often, sulking. I would put on a deep frown and stick out my lips and Mary would say dismissively, 'The wind will change one day and you'll be stuck like that,' or, alternatively, 'I could ride to London on your lips.' With so little reaction my tempers soon ran out of steam.

Our nursery life was a whole world, our soft toys our family, and Mary all we needed by way of a mother. It mattered not at all that our parents were remote. Every evening, after tea in the nursery (which, if we were lucky, consisted of toast made on the nursery fire, spread with Cook's best beef dripping and sprinkled with salt), Mary would prepare us for our ritual visit to the drawing-room, for which we were dressed in our best muslin frocks, white socks and bronze dancing pumps.

Mary would comb my ringlets round her finger while I squirmed and protested, 'Ow, you're hurting me!'

'Hold still child,' Mary would say through clenched teeth which held the clean hair-ribbon.

And I would vow silently, 'When I have children I'll *never* let them have ringlets. They're *cruel*!'

I never worked out for whose benefit the ringlets were meant to be.

Vanity was regarded as an arch-sin and we must never be told we looked pretty because that would make us vain. 'Who do you think is going to look at *you*?' was the standard put-down. Yet Mummy obviously liked it when other people made flattering remarks about my ringlets, though she pretended not to. Maybe this vicarious sort of vanity bent the rules sufficiently for it not to be regarded as sinful.

In the drawing-room one was on one's best behaviour. There was no roaring about – a few elegant dance steps to the gramophone might be allowed, but the drawing-room was no place to let off steam: there were too many delicate pieces of china and glass for that. Sometimes we would play games, Beggar-My-Neighbour or Snap, Hunt the Thimble or I-Spy. Sometimes one or other parent would read to us. We preferred Daddy's reading; Mummy was always skipping bits that she thought we wouldn't understand or were unsuitable and this led to a disjointed delivery that soon had our attention wandering. Daddy, on the other hand, read us blood-curdling stories from *Norse Fairy Tales* which had our attention riveted. I can see the book now, a thick, blue volume, faded and tatty from two whole generations of handling, and with scarey drawings of trolls with several heads wielding ferocious spiked clubs. Not, one might think, the stuff to go to bed on, but we loved it and applauded the marvellous audacity of its heroes:

'Fire and flame!' screamed the Troll.

'Fire and flame yourself,' said Shortshanks.

And it never seemed improbable that as soon as little boys were born they said to their mother, 'Give me my share of the inheritance, for I must go out into the world to seek my fortune.' Not unnaturally, the mother, poor woman, was somewhat reluctant to see the tiny mite set forth on his own. 'But the little one begged and prayed' until finally she packed his few belongings in a knapsack and off he went. 'He had not gone very far when . . . ' and there the story took off.

Honor disliked this hour when Pip and I claimed the attention of our parents. She thought it was all very childish and showed obvious signs of relief when, at exactly six o'clock, there was a tap on the door and Mary was there to whisk us off to bed.

Honor was not really a creature of the nursery as we were. All her life she had spent her time with Mummy and there was no doubting that those two enjoyed an unusually close relationship. Honor had been born in the early days of the marriage when our parents were hard up. She had been premature and delicate and during the first twelve months of her precarious existence the close bond had been forged which was to last a lifetime. But it caused a great divide to open up between us, and if Pip and I were never jealous of each other we were frantically jealous of Honor. Things went from bad to worse until there was almost open warfare between us. Honor had beautiful china dolls on which she doted and these dolls became the objects of our loathing and the villains of all our nursery play-acting. If we could capture one we would tie it to the table leg, cut its hair, poke its eyes in, break off fingers – just deserts, we fancied, for imagined wickednesses. These savage attacks always ended in tears and dolls were always having to be despatched to the dolls' hospital for mending. So a lock was fitted to the chest on the landing and the dolls were kept in there, out of our reach.

It was sad for Honor; she herself had been an intensely lonely child and had longed for brothers and sisters, a request for whom always headed her list for Father Christmas. But by the time playmates arrived the age gap was already too great. The fact that Pip and I became inseparable play-fellows and partners in crime made it even more unbearable for her, and we had to wait until we had children of our own for the rift to heal.

All this went right over the heads of our parents who were completely wrapped up in one another and now had the excitement of renovating and furnishing the house and turning the garden from a neglected Victorian wilderness into an elaborate formal garden. When they bought the house there had been no sign of the stone pediments over the front door and ground-floor windows, for the entire front had been enshrouded in an impenetrable mantle of ivy. Then my mother found an old picture postcard of the house in the village post office which showed the pediments before the ivy had taken over so completely. Feverishly my father set to work, with a ladder, strong secateurs and impatient hands, ripping and tugging and cutting until the pediments were gradually revealed. He might have been unearthing a pharaoh's tomb, it was so wildly exciting.

My maternal grandfather, Thomas H. Mawson, by this time a well-known landscape architect, was called in to redesign the four acres of garden and work on a large scale began almost straight away. I

Owls know better than to eat their neighbours' children

remember watching from the nursery window while a jolly little steam-roller laid the new gravel drive and being confined to the house while a tree stump was blow up with dynamite to make way for the flag path of York paving stones. Though the garden that eventually emerged (it took nearly twenty years) was generally regarded as an excellent example of Grandpa's work, I am glad that I can remember what it was like before work started.

On either side of the house was a wood of mature trees. These remained, of course. They were ash, beech, chestnut, witch-elm, sycamore and hornbeam and were home to some fifty pairs of rooks whose gentle cawing was to greet my waking moments for almost two decades. One large tree had more than its fair share of nests. The colony grew, year by year, until the nests merged into an enormous raft which could not be dismantled at the rooks' annual refurbishment. It became known as Fort Belvedere. In time, a pair of tawny owls took up residence in the 'basement' and the rooks used to chivvy them as they sat in the branches outside their front door, keeping half an eye on the world around them. But owls know better than to eat their neighbours' children and would wait until the hours of darkness to swoop silently on rustling mice below.

Looking for fairies in the wood

On the woodland floor beneath were carpets of snowdrops and aconites, celandines and bluebells, violets and wood sorrel. All trees are special to me but some, like people, have magnetic qualities that draw you to them. One of the pair of cedars which flanked the front gate had a family of red squirrels living in it. They were there for many years and we could watch their fascinating antics from the nursery window. Another curiosity was the very tall, straight ash tree standing sentinel by the back gate. The base of the tree spread out into the roots and made many mossy pockets where we were sure the fairies lived. It spread so much that first it bent the iron fence in front of it and, eventually, as the years went by, swallowed the fence up entirely until nothing was to be seen but strange wrinkles in the bark. Yet another favourite was a chestnut tree by the kitchen door that provided a strong, high branch perfect for bearing a swing. That swing provided us with a splendid combination of pleasure, skill, exercise, excitement and danger for a great many years. We became great exponents and took some enormous risks, but nothing disastrous ever happened.

The rest of the garden was a green expanse of lawns, running away into meadow, orchard or copse, and old brick walls hanging with curtains of ivy. There was a fairy dell and old arbours of larch poles and trellis covered with rambling roses and, best of all, a rustic summerhouse, its romantic thatched roof trailing with rampant *Clematis montana* in which a song thrush made its nest every year. It was a garden full of secrets and surprises, full of hiding places and adventures. And, of course, it was an ideal place for the fairies, signs of whom Pip and I would regularly observe all over the place.

Most of that was to change. The large unfettered lawn was regimented into straight lines, herbaceous borders, rose beds, yew hedges and a tennis court. 'Vistas' opened up here and there, leading the eye to a pergola, sundial, statue, or garden seat. We were told to be careful not to tread on the neat, clipped grass edges, or to let our ball go into the flower beds. The fairy dell was demolished, the stones carted away one by one to build a wall (*another* straight line). But worse was to come. The summerhouse was chopped up for firewood to make way for an ornamental fish pond surrounded by a paved garden. The grassy slope where the moon daisies grew, which we used to hurtle down to the summerhouse, became another wall with a flight of brick steps in it. In fact, my father did a good deal of the work himself and developed a passion for bricklaying which lasted for years. No sooner was a wall finished than he was ready to start on gate piers, or a pond, a flight of steps, an archway or a gazebo. There was no stopping him.

Though these changes were the work of Grandpa, I was fortunately unaware of his implication in the destruction of my wilderness. Not that knowing would have changed my feelings towards him. I loved him dearly and the best part of the alterations to the garden was that he came over on regular visits from his home near Lancaster and stayed two or three weeks at a time. There are very few adults who can communicate with children on their own level and, without being patronizing, give them their full attention even when there are other people around. I only knew three such people in my childhood and Grandpa was one of them.

Like me, he believed in fairies and shared my unexpressed belief that the average grown-up had a very blinkered view of the possibilities that lie beyond the *real* world. What is real? Reality relates in some way to experience. A child with little experience of 'the real world' fills in the gaps with a fertile imagination, which is simply a very real experience in the head. Grandpa imagined beautiful gardens in his head, just as a composer imagines music. Then he was clever enough to create them. Was it any more real on the ground than it had been in his head? Is music in a composer's mind less real than the notes on the page? We are bidden, on pain of eternal damnation, to believe in angels and archangels and all the company of Heaven, in Virgin birth, Holy Ghost and Resurrection. Why draw the line at fairies? Yet once, when I was prattling on about fairies, a visitor said to my mother, 'That child is a liar. What are you going to do about it?'

When Grandpa and I went walking in the wood, hand in hand, looking for fairies or anything else of mutual interest, there was seldom much need to talk. He would point with his stick to something which had caught his eye – a cobweb bespangled with dew, a sprouting sycamore seedling, a bird's feather beautifully marked – and there we were, just the two of us, in a secret and enchanted kingdom. Fairies or no fairies, with Grandpa's help I learned a great deal about how to look at the wonders of the world we live in and to catch a glimpse of what lies beyond.

In Service

In Service

Some inaccurate nonsense is still talked about domestic service in 'the good old days', as though it were a disgraceful form of exploitation and slavery. Undoubtedly, there were bad employers in that field as in every other, but service has to be measured against the general standards of employment at that time. Work was hard and physical, hours were long and pay was low whether one worked on the land, in a factory, or in domestic service. The social structure was unfair but that's the way it was.

In the country districts of North Lincolnshire girls did not have much choice. There was the jam factory at Brigg and the bicycle factory at Barton. Country shops were mostly run by their owners and their families and did not employ labour. That left domestic service or work on the land. Mothers were usually reluctant to let their daughters work on the land because, they said, it made them coarse. They became rough mannered, picked up bad language from the men and stood a greater risk of 'getting into trouble', as pregnancy was always called. Nor did they learn anything which was going to be of use to them in later life.

So service had a good deal to commend it and if a girl could be placed in one of the larger houses which employed five or six staff there was a proper career structure. Starting maybe as a kitchen-maid she would arrive, a brave fourteen straight from school, with her mother's words of admonition ringing in her ears and all her worldly possessions in a tin trunk with a handle at each end and a rounded top like a pirate's treasure chest. It had to be rounded to accommodate her Sunday hat, wide-brimmed and decorated with buttercups and daisies or, if like Ivy her father happened to be a game-keeper, some rather exotic feathers.

A kitchen-maid's work was especially hard. Her hands were always in water, from the moment of scrubbing the front door steps at seven in the morning to washing up after the evening meal. Before the days of detergents, rubber gloves or dishwashers, raw soda crystals were the only aid to washing up and hands were almost permanently sore and chapped, making contact with salt or lemon juice excruciatingly painful. One remedy was to rub the hands with warm mutton fat and go to bed wearing cotton gloves. Edna, the kitchen-maid, once confided that kneading the bread was the best way to get your hands clean.

Nevertheless, there were compensations. She would enjoy an excellent diet at a time when many families' idea of meat seldom went beyond fat bacon, and she probably had a bed to herself for the first time in her life. And it was in the kitchen that she became cook's understudy, with enough insight into the job to decide whether she wished one day to become a cook, with a kitchen-maid to do her dirty work for her (ah! that was real power, that was!), or whether her aim was to become head housemaid by the time she married.

The difficulties of finding employment being what they were, my mother considered it her social duty to employ as many staff as she could afford. In the early days at Thornton, while Pip and I were still in the nursery, that consisted of butler, cook, kitchen-maid, under-housemaid, head housemaid, parlour-maid, nanny and nursery-maid. My mother would never have a girl come to the house to be interviewed but preferred to see the girl in her own home where it was easy to tell by the standards maintained whether the mother herself had been in service.

George Hibberd joined us as butler almost as soon as we moved in. He had been in service all his life and had worked his way up from boot-boy to become valet to the First Gentleman of the King's Wardrobe, which required him to be at Buckingham Palace, Windsor, Scotland, or to travel on state visits abroad. When the war came he enlisted and became my father's batman. Whatever he may have had planned for the future fell apart when his young wife died in the influenza epidemic of 1918, leaving him with an infant son who was brought up by his sister. All George wanted was to spend the rest of his life looking after my father and his household – a job he did supremely well until his death forty-five years later.

Although he enjoyed the title of butler – the top rank in the household hierarchy – he was in fact general factotum, boot-boy, boiler-man, footman, chauffeur, valet and keeper of the 'privy purse'. When one of the family was catching a train George would be there to say, 'Have you enough small change for a taxi, a cup of tea, a newspaper and tips?' This was a particularly valuable service for my mother who seldom got round to such details and had been known to head for the station clutching toast and marmalade in one hand and a pair of shoes in the other. A note of the debt would be pencilled in on the edge of the calendar in George's pantry to be cleared at the end of the month. Beside the calendar hung a photograph of George himself as a young footman in some ducal household – resplendent in powdered wig, braided coat, satin knee-breeches, white stockings and shoes with big silver buckles. As a child I could well believe that up until the moment the Fairy Godmother had waved her wand he had been a lizard.

George's pantry was a warm and friendly place – warm because the boiler lived there and friendly because George himself, though a man of few words and very quietly spoken, was endlessly good-humoured and patient. We loved to seek his company and his pantry was full of special things. The glass, the best china and the silver were never allowed to go into the kitchen but were always washed by George personally, this being done in an old, much used, much scoured, wooden tub.

When the big doors of the china cupboard were open we could catch a glimpse of beautiful things on the top shelf that only came out at Christmas. And on a lower shelf was a large, square, baize-lined basket containing the table silver in daily use.

The silver was George's special pride and joy. After washing, the spoons and forks were put to stand in a jug of boiling water that contained a little whitening. They were then placed carefully in rows on a cotton cloth on the wooden draining board and another jug of boiling water was poured over them before they were dried and rubbed up with a soft shammy-leather. Very rarely was it necessary to clean them with polish.

Another of George's tasks was to train parlour-maids in the finesse of waiting at table. This he did to perfection. An unobtrusive decorum was the hallmark of good dining-room work and George would put a new girl through her paces, with little more than good example, a look or a nod (very seldom a whisper), until she had mastered all the intricacies required – such as how to offer vegetable dishes (one in each hand) on the proper side, holding the dishes securely without showing her thumbs. You had to have considerable nerve and self-confidence to be a good parlour-maid.

The two of them waited at table for lunch and dinner but never at breakfast (that being a 'flexi-time' meal). Food punctuated the day at regular intervals and, although we seemed to eat a prodigious amount, we were always hungry. The food was filling rather than rich, with much less sugar than is nowadays consumed and cream a rarity reserved for special occasions. Nobody in our household was fat. We led energetic lives and needed the calories to keep out the cold in a virtually unheated house. Often in wintertime our face-flannels were frozen stiff as boards in the morning.

Breakfast was a lovely meal. My father had already left for work by the time we put in an appearance at eight o'clock, and there, on the sideboard with its hotplate, was porridge or stewed fruit, bacon with eggs or tomatoes, mushrooms, kidneys and the like. There were sausages on Sundays and always fish on Fridays: home-made fish cakes, kedgeree, or smoked haddock poached in milk with poached eggs. Toast and marmalade rounded things off very nicely and kept the wolf from the door until elevenses, when a tray appeared with glasses of milk and gingerbread.

Lunch was a plain, filling meal which relied on a great deal of suet – dumplings and steamed puddings. But again Fridays were always fish days and it is not surprising that, engaged in the fishing industry as my father was, fish always figured largely and many ingenious ways were found of cooking it. One favourite – a Lincolnshire speciality I believe – was a whole haddock (some 10 or 12 lbs of it) stuffed with breadcrumbs, lemon and parsley, roasted in the oven and served with a rich brown gravy. From time to time we became guinea pigs for early experiments in deep-frozen and pre-cooked fish. I remember my father once asking everyone at the table what they thought of the halibut they had just eaten. It was delicious! 'Eighteen months in the cold store!' my father declared triumphantly.

Tea, at half-past four, was always lavish. Plum bread, wafer-thin sandwiches with crusts removed and decorated with sprigs of parsley, scones, fruit cake and an iced cake. Where did we put it all? And on Saturdays there were always round bread buns, hot from the oven, their tops all crisp and crunchy, and dripping with butter. They were a knockout.

Dinner was an altogether grander occasion that we children knew nothing about. At half-past seven precisely George emerged from his pantry into the hall with the big brass gong, on which he beat a resounding tattoo that echoed through the house. It was to warn the grown-ups that it was time to change, and on the stroke of eight the gong rang out again, this time for dinner. The ladies wore long frocks in chiffons and silks, sometimes trimmed with fur, sometimes weighed down with sewn-on beads, making them sparkle in the soft candle-light and swing when they walked. Their clothes had been carefully laid out for them on their beds by the housemaids. My father wore a dinner-jacket every night of his life (except Sundays) until the outbreak of the Second World War, and black patent-leather slippers with flat, tailored bows on the toes. George exercised meticulous care over my father's clothes. Mummy once said to him, 'George, has the master any old clothes for the jumble sale?' and got the reply, 'Yes, madam, but he wears them all!'

George and Cook ruled the roost in the servants' hall. It was their kingdom and totally out of bounds to us except on the rarest occasions. Every morning immediately after breakfast my mother went down to the servants' hall to order the menus for the day. Occasionally one of us children might be allowed to accompany her. The scene was always the same. Cook in her clean, starched cap and apron, a fire burning in the grate in wintertime, everything spick and span and Mummy seated at the head of the table in the high-backed Windsor chair, the order book open at the right day on the table in front of her, with pink pages and a pencil attached by a piece of string. She and Cook would discuss the meals for the days ahead, how to dispose of left-overs, what fruit and vegetables the gardener had brought in and what items needed to be re-ordered from the grocer. A red-letter day for us children was the arrival of a new consignment of candied peel because we were given the lumps of candy sugar from the hollow of each segment of peel. Flour came in large sacks and was tipped into a big metal bin in the kitchen from whence it was dug out with a scoop. All our bread was made at home, twice a week, twelve loaves at a time. When they were rising in their tins, placed in a row along the steel fender in front of the range, they looked like so many new-born babies in tiny cots.

Monday mornings saw all hands to the task of wash-day. The girls rose at five-thirty and stood on duck-boarding at the long table in the laundry, on which were three square wooden wash-tubs, each with a little shelf across the corner to hold the soap. And there they rubbed and scrubbed till by breakfast time the drying ground was already billowing with the first batch of sheets and pillow-cases. Some items of washing required the dolly-tub – a round barrel made of corrugated zinc in which a strange wooden device known as a dolly-peg was used to agitate the clothes against the corrugations. It was heavy work and developed strong arm and shoulder muscles. Then, of course, there was the copper, with a fire underneath, in which whites were boiled. And everything went through the mangle, the water running on to the stone-flagged floor and out through a drain in the wall. Hence the need for the duck-boarding. When the dry washing had been brought in Pip and I would search the long grass for clothes pegs which we bartered with Cook for sugar-lumps.

Some people entrusted their washing to house-bound labourers' wives, who were glad of the chance to earn a shilling or two in their own homes. But often they did not have the price of a clothes-line and would spread the washing out over the hawthorn hedges instead, which didn't do it much good. In our household we imported Mrs Copeland to help on Mondays. She was a stout, jolly lady with a round, red face and her wispy hair pinned up in a bun on the top of her head. She had enormous arms, as thick as thighs, with deep dimples in the elbows. Mrs Copeland reigned expertly over the copper, standing there, enveloped in steam, lifting and turning the whites with the copper-stick. She was immensely strong.

Ironing was done on Tuesdays. With no ironing-boards and no electric irons the work was done on a large table with a relay of flat irons of different shapes and sizes which lived permanently in the bottom oven of the kitchen range. The girls had two methods of testing the heat of the iron. One was to spit on it and judge the heat by the pitch of the fizz it made – the higher the hotter – the other, more daring and dangerous, was to hold the iron up very close to the cheek. There must have been many near misses, but I can't remember anyone actually burning themselves.

The first duty of the morning for the housemaids was to call the adults in the house with a tray of tea. The knock on the door came at seven o'clock precisely; the curtains were drawn back neatly and the little tea-tray, with its pretty china (especially designed and sold as an early morning tea-set), put down on the bedside table. This was followed some minutes later by a big brass jug of hot water for washing, which was placed in the dressing-room and covered with a towel to keep it hot until it was required. The head housemaid had charge of the linen-room where she mended and had a sewing machine for turning sheets sides-to-middle when they wore thin.

It was one of the parlour-maid's duties to make the bees-wax furniture polish. Soap and bees-wax were grated on a cheese grater into a large jam-jar and covered with pure turpentine. The jar was then put on the side of the kitchen range and stirred occasionally over a period of several days until the ingredients had become blended into a smooth cream. The bees-wax was from our own hives which were kept against the kitchen garden wall. I remember very little about them, except when they swarmed. This generated a good deal of excitement, with people rushing about dressed in extraordinary garb. If they swarmed on one of our own fruit trees they could easily be shaken off into a box and retrieved. But on one occasion the swarm took off over the fields towards the village in an erratic black cloud pursued by Daddy and Margie Swallow, our governess, ringing a handbell. The law said, so I was told, that the swarm was yours so long as you could keep it in sight, but once you lost sight of it anybody could claim it. So my memory retains a picture of the little black cloud gradually becoming invisible and of two figures growing smaller and smaller as they legged it at top speed across the paddock and Duddings Field, the sound of the bell wafting faintly and still more faintly on the breeze. Despite their best endeavours they lost the swarm and returned some time later, weary and mud-spattered.

Once a year a great domestic upheavel was enacted: this was spring-cleaning. After months of continuous fires and muddy boots, short days and long nights, a fever gripped the household staff as the first buds greened in the garden, lambs frolicked in the field and March winds swept winter away. Although spring-cleaning took an arduous three weeks or so, the maids always enjoyed the break with routine. First there was the visit from the sweep, who arrived, with his

Wash day

young assistant, in a donkey cart bristling with brushes and bundles of rods. With ten or more chimneys to be swept, and the ground floor fires three whole storeys from their respective pots, it required a long day's work and a phenomenal length of connecting rods to do the job. But he was a jolly man who sang and cracked jokes as he worked and, so he told Pip and me, played the cello in the local amateur orchestra. We found him good company, and there was the excitement of rushing out on to the lawn to see the brush come out at the top. At the end of the day the prodigious amount of soot was piled up against the wall by the greenhouse, waiting to be used on the garden.

Carpets were folded and carried outside where they were draped over the washing-line, one by one, and given a hearty beating with a special carpet beater, a flat object woven from twisted willow or basket-cane. Then the girls dragged the carpets up and down the grass, first back-side down to remove the dust and then reversed to bring up the pile. All this was accompanied by a great deal of fooling about and laughter.

An important part of the ritual was whitewashing the ceilings, always darkened and marked by the paraffin lamps. 'Doing the tops' it was referred to and most people did their own. But our ceilings were 13 ft high so decorators were brought in for the task. In those days there were always plenty of local tradesmen and odd-job men to call upon at such times.

There was in our village an old lady called Grannie Smith who lived to be 102. When she was well into her nineties my mother met her hurrying down the village street in apron and head-scarf, and carrying a large bucket.

'Hello, Grannie Smith,' my mother said, 'Where are you off to in such a hurry?'

'Oh, I'm going to help my daughter do her tops. I don't like her standing on the ladder. She's over seventy, you know!'

Spring-cleaning was also the time when cupboards and drawers were turned out, occasional china given a wash and all the linen not in regular use laundered to stop it from going yellow. But finally everything was finished. The house gleamed and sparkled and had a special smell. And it took ages to find all our toys, games and books again.

Maids came and went and I remember Cathleen, Queenie, Rose, Ada, Edith, Edna, Mabel and Ivy with affection. We did not have close contact with them, except on Mary's day out when they would step into the breach and teach us singing games, skipping and suchlike. I remember Rose teaching me to swing a milk can of water round and round over my head without the water spilling. She also taught me to sew, threading and rethreading my needle with infinite patience until I mastered it. Edna, the kitchen-maid, used to borrow Cook's pince-nez spectacles on her day out because she thought they suited her, although she could hardly see a yard in front of her face in them. Cathleen sometimes regaled us with lurid tales of her rather disreputable neighbours and would tell us how the old grannie would go out into the back yard, step out of her knickers, put them under the pump and hang them on the line. Later in the day she would take them off the line and step back into them. Such risqué stories were never to be repeated in front of the grown-ups, of course. Knickers were, needless to say, quite unmentionable and Queenie would say disapprovingly, 'You shouldn't tell them things like that.'

Mary was the mainstay of our young lives. A local girl with no formal child-care training, she preferred not to be called nanny. She wore no uniform other than a crisp white apron with a bib top and straps that crossed at the back. Although I cannot remember Mary playing with us or reading to us or suggesting things we might do, she was an all-pervading presence, quiet, calm, supportive and *always there*. As Mary was on her own without the help of a Minnie Hank there was plenty to do. Pip and I would be playing with our family of soft toys, dressing and undressing them, running schools and hospitals and picnics for 'the children', and Mary would be tackling a pile of ironing while we bombarded her with our comments and questions, seeking to draw her into our play. 'Wasn't it, Mary?' or 'Shall we, Mary?', and without lifting her head Mary would reply 'M–hm!' or 'M–hm?' and we would be quite content that we had received the appropriate answer. She was probably thinking of her boyfriend, Walter the butcher's boy, a cheery, apple-cheeked, curly-headed scamp whom she eventually married. It was Walter who undoubtedly got the better of the bargain. And like all other girls of her age, Mary had a 'bottom drawer' where she collected things for the day when she had a home of her own. The bottom drawer was a very serious affair and into it went little gifts received at birthdays and Christmas, odd useful things picked up at jumble sales and a great many home-made items such as aprons and cushion-covers, table-cloths and pillow-cases made out of the best parts of worn-out sheets.

'What are you doing, Mary?' we would ask.

'It's for my bottom drawer,' Mary would answer, with considerable pride.

Grown-ups in our household carried on a conspiracy against us typified by the remark, *sotto voce*, 'Not in front of the children.' It meant that for most of the time we were either dangerously naïve or morbidly curious – and frequently both. There was one simply awful occasion when the youngest child of a family we knew was killed in an accident. He was five, and a week or two prior to the accident he had been over to play with us sporting the most colourful black eye, which fascinated me because I had never seen a black eye before. We were not told of Nigel's death, but on the day of the funeral his brothers came to spend the day with us. I said innocently, 'How's Nigel's eye?' and Derek answered, 'What do you mean, how's Nigel's eye? Nigel's dead. The last time I saw him his face was all covered with blood.'

The shock-waves of Derek's words haunt me yet. It was unforgiveable and totally unnecessary that we had been left so dangerously uninformed. But when I thought about it afterwards I could remember a lot of whisperings and 'not in front of the children' which our fertile imaginations and long ears had misconstrued as having something to do with Mrs Tilley's new twins.

We lived in a cocooned world where nothing nasty or frightening was ever supposed to happen – that was only in storybooks – where underclothes could not be mentioned outside the nursery and bodily functions didn't exist. Grown-ups lived a curious life of pretence. They pretended not to notice certain lapses of etiquette, they pretended to like people they did not like and to find their conversation amusing when it was boring. It was all part of 'good manners', which were taken to extraordinary lengths. For instance, my mother always wore a ridiculous hat when someone was coming to tea.

'Where are you going, Mummy?'

'I'm not going anywhere.'

'Then why are you wearing a hat?'

'Because Miss Robertson is coming to tea.'

'But why are you wearing a hat?'

'Because Miss Robertson will be wearing a hat.'

In a sense I envied the cottage children (with whom we were not supposed to play in case we caught things in our heads) because, for all their poverty, they had a marvellous reality about them. When one large family had to exist in one living-room and one bedroom 'not in front of the children' was an impossibility. They knew about birth and death and illness and bodily functions and took them all in their stride. Mary was friendly with Mrs Bratby who lived in one of the cottages down the road from us and occasionally we would go in while they had a chat. There were five Bratby children. Ruby, the eldest, was a spontaneously kind and outgoing girl and very much a second mother to the younger ones. Mr Bratby was cowman at the farm and their poverty was measured by the fact that the younger children wore neither shoes nor knickers. I remember Mrs Bratby complaining indignantly to Mary that the youngest girl had been sent home from school with a note that she should not attend again unless she wore knickers. 'She's nobbut a little bairn: what harm is there in it?' It was as though the child herself had been rejected for the very flimsiest of reasons.

The insides of the cottages always intrigued us; they were so utterly different from anything we knew at home. In nearly every one there was a rag rug in front of the fire, a product of one of the most distinctive of the thrift crafts, made of strips of old material worked into a sacking base with a hook. Mostly the rugs reflected the dark, practical clothes people wore, predominantly black and navy, but sometimes great skill and flair went into the designs and patterns would appear in bright colours – reds, blues, greens. Oh, how I wanted a rag rug!

The other thing about the cottages was that they always had an interesting smell. Sometimes it was new bread or boiled fat bacon. More often it was washing drying round the fire. What did one do when it rained and there were five children and only one room? While Mary and Mrs Bratby talked we would stand there like dummies, eyeing the Bratby children and being eyed back, never a muscle moving nor a word exchanged. One day the smell of drying clothes was permeated by another warm and unmistakably pungent aroma. Mrs Bratby's nose twitched. 'Pooh! Teddy, is that you farted? Go to the closet and don't come back until you've done it.' Teddy, very red, slunk out to the privy at the bottom of the garden while Pip and I stood rooted to the spot, wide-eyed and open-mouthed. But we learnt something of the real world that day.

The strictures that discouraged us from playing with the village children did not, fortunately, apply to the gardener's family. Mr and Mrs Watson had five daughters, all named after plants, and Olive, the youngest and one year my senior, was my regular playmate. Often I would wend my way through the wood to the cottage attached to the stables. It was a lovely cottage with roses round the door, variegated ivy on the wall, and a lush green fern growing in the damp shade at the base of the water butt.

'Can Olive play?' I would ask. Sometimes she would and sometimes she wouldn't. Sometimes I could wheedle my way into the cottage where the big attraction was a musical clock on the mantlepiece over the kitchen range which chimed a pretty little tune on the hour. I remember it clearly; it went like this:

Olive knew games which we didn't know, and a method of picking 'it' which I have never come across since:

'As I was going down icky-picky lane
I met some icky-picky people.
What colour were they dressed in?'
'Blue.' [or whatever]
'B – L – U – E spells blue
So out you must go.'

She was also adept at skipping and the stable yard was a good place to practise 'salt and pepper' and the intricacies of running into a rope turned by two other people. This skill had tricky refinements as when the rope-turners themselves turned in to jump the rope while still keeping it turning.

When Olive couldn't play I liked nothing better than to be with Watson in the garden. He was a small, bird-like man with bright, observant eyes and boundless energy. He worked all the hours of daylight and, when daylight was in short supply, was to be seen, morning and evening, tending his greenhouses by the light of a storm-lantern. His brisk step along the path was accompanied by a tuneless 'Pom pa-pom pa-pom', so that I knew just where to find him, and I would plague him with endless questions – about himself, what he was doing, why he was doing it and generally what made the world go round. He was very patient with me. 'I'm called Thomas Andrew. Two apostles they were. You can't do much better than that, now can you?' But finally I always went too far, taking up his time and trying his patience, or asking questions he was not prepared to answer.

'Why is Jap shut up? Why does she want puppies? Why don't you want her to have puppies? Puppies would be nice.'

And Watson would say, 'I can't stay here talking to you all day. I've got work to do.'

And he'd be off – 'Pom pa-pom pa-pom' – and I knew that enough was enough. But he was never sharp with me and sometimes I would be allowed to help in some way, preparing a seed-tray and sowing my very own seeds, or taking cuttings from the antirrhinum plants. I learned to love the smell and feel of the earth and the delicate sensation of handling tiny plants. To this day I cannot wear gardening gloves because to my mind they dull the message that passes from the soil to the brain via the hands. Maybe 'brain' is too clinical a word, just as 'soul' would be too emotive. But what does one call that innate spark which inhabits every living thing and binds us into one 'Earth family'?

The life of leisure thrust upon her by a well-ordered staff cannot have come easily to my mother. Used as she was to a large, lively and cultured family and a wide circle of friends, a small village in rural Lincolnshire must have seemed a desert. With my father at work all day there were many hours of loneliness that were difficult to fill with useful employment. It was not done to lend a hand in the house or the kitchen. I remember having a great desire to learn how to darn socks and iron my own clothes, but my mother reproved me gently with 'You mustn't take work away from a girl who really *needs* the job.'

Her artistic flair surfaced here and there in such activities as flower-arranging, at which she became adept and for which she grew rows of flowers for cutting in the vegetable garden. Larkspur, gypsophila and love-in-a-mist shone out brightly from a green sea of cabbages, lettuces and carrot-tops, and there was always a tall row of sweet-peas (my mother's favourite) nearby. The house was full of flowers and from every room there emanated a gentle fragrance.

Two factors made my mother's life tolerable. One was the great love my parents had for one another, which never diminished in all the years of their married life. The other was the companionship of her beloved sister, Tassie, who lived with us, and the laughter they shared. As they talked things over together and discussed my mother's frustrated desire for an artistic outlet of her own, a spark of an idea began to formulate itself which was eventually to grow into an extraordinarily successful enterprise.

During her search for maids and with it her growing knowledge of local families, my mother had come across several girls who were in some way too delicate or disabled to find employment in service or on the land. One girl was epileptic, another had a deformed and shortened leg, a third suffered severely from asthma. A room was set aside as a workroom and these girls came every day to learn handicrafts from my mother. A small range of saleable goods, designed (and the prototypes made) by my mother, soon established a viable production line. Such items as quilted knitting bags and cushion-covers, tea-trays with embroidered panels to display under glass and tea cosies were made to a highly professional standard and sold in aid of the Red Cross, which was still coping with the aftermath of the war. My mother's favourite contribution to the work was the modelling of sprays of delicate, china-like flowers, realistically painted and attached to such items as dressing-table mirrors. At first she used bread dough until she found a supply of more suitable material.

Though my mother was the mainspring of ideas and design in the early days, she was no businesswoman and would happily have given the products away. But Tassie, who had less artistic ability of her own, proved to be something of a genius when it came to marketing and between them they made a perfect team. The business grew and prospered, became known as Thornton Industries and, as the work was pleasant, in pleasant surroundings, it was not long before able-bodied girls were knocking at the door seeking employment. Finally, over thirty girls were employed in spacious workrooms over the stables, supplying leading shops all over the country.

Tassie was in her element, travelling for the firm, meeting people, exuding charm and making friends wherever she went, humping suitcases of samples about until the day when a permanent London showroom was established.

When my father's business ran into difficulties and big changes had to be made necessitating the borrowing of large sums of money and a general tightening of belts at home, it was my mother's work that kept the roof over our heads. Nothing was said to us children, of course, but one day I overheard a friend of my mother's say, 'I hear you're selling Thornton.' The cold hand of panic gripped my stomach and my mother, seeing the anguish on my face said hurriedly, 'Oh, no, no! It won't come to that,' and the conversation was changed abruptly. After that I kept noticing ominous signs. My mother put in long hours in the workroom and some of the things we had taken for granted – new toys, clothes, outings – were no longer readily available. But the storm was eventually weathered and there were good times ahead.

Maiden Aunts

Maiden Aunts

'I always told you I wasn't well' would have been a suitable epitaph for my Aunt Millicent. Mint, as everybody called her, enjoyed bad health in her latter years. Her sister Dolly, faithful, loving and long-suffering, would support her as she detailed her symptoms to anyone who would listen.

'Oh, I *was* ill, wasn't I, Dolly?'

'Oh, she *was*. In all my experience I have *never* seen *anybody* suffer as she did.'

Which prompted more of the same.

It wasn't always like that and I like to think of her in happier times, when life seemed as if it might hold nice surprises – a handsome prince, for example. Mint had always brightened the scene with a colourful line in exaggeration – 'My dear, without a word of a lie, as I stand here, the *biggest* . . .!' Grown-ups are such cynics, but in our youth, before we knew what a pinch of salt was for, our eyes would glisten as we entered her magic land. For close companion to the overstatement is a fertile imagination and Mint's imagination made her a favourite visitor at our house. There would be story-telling, dressing-up and play-acting, inventing dances to gramophone music, picnics and expeditions into the unknown: pirates, shipwrecks and desert islands; witches and spells and fairy lands forlorn. There was a sort of tacit understanding that Mint could play all the leading parts – especially the baddies – provided all the games had happy endings, on which Pip and I insisted. If Mint wanted the roses to fall down and die at the end of a Mendelssohn overture then Pip and I would stand our ground and there was absolutely *nothing doing*. It was useless for Mint to wheedle, 'But roses *do* die at the end of the summer.' Not in our book they didn't.

That was the best thing about maiden aunts – they had *time*. Parents seldom had time, though why they did not is hard to imagine. The house was full of servants and there ought to have been time for everything they wanted to do. Maybe that was it. They did what they wanted and that did not include encouraging the children to be wild and noisy and play games that would certainly end in tears – if not nightmares. Lord, what dull lives grown-ups led!

Mint was the youngest of a family of nine. Grannie Mawson once told me, 'I wouldn't have had nine children if I had known how *not* to, but, having got them, which ones would I do without?' A lady of remarkable character and philosophy, she reared her large brood on a shoe-string with much love and common sense and discipline. Of the four daughters my mother, the eldest, was the only one to marry, and that was before the First World War.

It seemed to me in those far-off days of the 1920s that every family had a good supply of maiden aunts to call upon in times of trouble. They would come when the measles broke out, or when parents were called away, and would stay for a month or more. That was the way families were constructed by God, who understood the intricacies of these matters and the necessity for maiden aunts. It only gradually dawned on me, many years later, that the potential husbands of these sad and useful ladies had been killed in the war and that they were not single from choice, nor from God's good planning, but because there were not enough men to go round.

Auntie Dolly had nursed her terribly wounded fiancé back to health but a week after returning to the trenches he was killed. She was as faithful to his memory as she would have been to him in life and all thoughts of husband, home and family were tenderly and quietly packed away into the back of her mind so that she could get on with her life of caring for others. Aunt Frances, whom we always called Tassie, was vivacious and beautiful with a passionate nature and the greenest eyes I have ever seen. She could undoubtedly have found herself a husband, except that she was always waiting for something better to turn up. An admiral or a lord or even a famous writer, would have done nicely. But she was not so much a spinster as a bachelor-girl and led an adventurous life, travelling abroad and driving a car long before it was usual for women to do so. Of the three maiden aunts only Mint deeply resented her spinsterhood. Her dressing-table was adorned with signed photos of her might-have-beens, who faded away because she was too keen. That didn't stop her from telling us that an engagement was about to be announced.

And she did her best, managing to dress up to the minute on her small allowance. When cloche hats, long beads and short skirts were in fashion Mint was the first to sport them – in shorter short skirts and longer long beads. And she could Tango and Charleston impressively.

Mint stayed at home and looked after her parents, Auntie Dolly continued with her nursing career and Tassie came to live more or less permanently with us – more or less, because she never stayed in one place for very long. She and my mother, close in age, were inseparable and entirely complementary in character; my mother cool, private, funny, Tassie living on the edge of her emotions.

As time went on Tassie and I developed a very special relationship. While Pip was still a baby and slept with Nanny in the night nursery, my small bed was alongside Tassie's big four-poster into which I would creep in the early morning. In the evening I would watch her dress for dinner and thought it very glamorous to wear a long evening dress, a pearl necklace and a velvet ribbon round her hair. Then she would kiss me goodnight and her perfume would linger in the darkness. As my eyes grew accustomed to the dark, through the partly open door I could make out a small shaft of light from the Kelly lamp on the landing, just enough to throw shadows on the ceiling from the carved top of the wardrobe. There were faces there, like kings and queens on playing cards – rather angular – and I would fall asleep thinking of stories in which they could play leading roles, as befitted such royal personages.

It was Tassie who introduced me to wildlife and to birds in particular. She was not a great expert but her enthusiasm was catching and she was very encouraging, giving me my first bird books, T.A. Coward's *Birds of the British Isles*. Hours and hours were spent poring over the illustrations and committing to memory the distinguishing features of each bird, its eggs and its name. Not that I always got the name right. There is a bird called a pratincole which I have never seen and am never likely to see. But I know what it looks like and as a child, steeped in Greek mythology and *Tales of the Gods and Heroes*, I pronounced it to myself as Pra-*tin*-co-lee – to rhyme with Penelope.

Maiden aunts would come when the measles broke out

Coward's books opened a wonderful door for me and each spring brought with it a sort of ecstasy of identifying bird-song, of finding the nests and watching the drama unfold. As I became older, eight or nine maybe, Tassie introduced me to Gilbert White's *History of Selborne*, reading it aloud to me each night when I was in bed. And together she and I joined the British Empire Naturalists' Association (known as BENA) which had a strong branch in our neighbourhood organized by John Davey, farmer and ornithologist extraordinary. This gave us access to their early morning rambles in local woods in spring. The members were very patient and helpful with the only child in the group and I felt very privileged. It was there that I first heard the sound of a great spotted woodpecker drumming, saw a little owl (still quite a rarity then), discovered by myself a mallard's nest in a clump of kingcups and thrilled to the song of the nightingale, whose nest in a low box bush was found by another member of the group. Many people have heard the nightingale; very few have seen those beautiful green-bronze eggs as I have done. I shall never forget.

Auntie Dolly came into my life in a very special way a few years later when, after an unusually hot summer, I went down with a severe bout of polio, with complications from which I nearly died. Maiden aunt to the rescue once more – Auntie Dolly gave up her job as a nursing sister to come and nurse me at home. There were no medical gadgets then, no antibiotics, no iron lung, no drip-feeding, no monitoring machines. It was 'hands-on' nursing of the very highest order that saved my life and of that there is absolutely no doubt at all.

Sundays

Sundays

Sunday was easily the best day of the week. It was different and special, getting off to a good start with sausages for breakfast, and Pip and I were allowed to come down to the dining-room for all meals. Daddy was always in a good mood, joking and teasing us – in fact it was clearly understood that *everybody* was in a good mood on Sunday *because* it was Sunday.

Mummy, who was not good at getting up in the morning, would arrive late as usual, entering the dining-room with a little pirouette and singing, 'Good morning, my dears'. She was usually equipped with a brilliant little excuse for being late. One morning it was, 'I dreamt I was at the dentist and every time I tried to get up he gave me another whiff of gas.' Daddy, who was her best audience, laughed and said, 'You're wonderful!'

Sometimes, when the weather was good, we walked the half mile to church, taking the short cut across Duddings Field and negotiating the two kissing gates. But it was more usual to go in the old brown open Buick. Once again Mummy was always late because she could never estimate how long it would take to do the things she wanted to do, such as arrange flowers for the dinner table. And as we sat in the car and waited Daddy would look at his watch and tap the steering wheel with impatient fingers. But the nearest he ever came to criticism was the remark, 'Your mother never wastes any of her *own* time.'

The ancient parish church of St Lawrence was large and handsome and towered over the rather mean rows of brick cottages and the Thornton Hunt Inn, which together comprised Thornton's one and only village street. Inside were massive pillars, Norman arches, wide aisles and a huge open space behind the pews where stood the chief glory of the church, a black Tournai marble font. One of only seven such fonts in England, its four square sides were adorned with writhing griffins, foliage, strange winged beasts and birds, all intricately intertwined and reminiscent of early illuminated manuscripts.

The font dates in all probability from the early twelfth century and is thus contemporary with the present church. Such a rare and costly item would surely have been the gift of some rich benefactor and it is possible that it was donated by the founder, William Albermarle, Earl of Holderness, who is himself buried in a Tournai marble tomb in Bridlington Priory. Not that I knew anything of that as a child, but there was never any doubt in my mind that the generations who had come and gone in that venerable building had left an aura behind them. All of them had been touched by the church at significant points on their earthly journey – baptism, marriage, burial – and all had shared with the church their joys as well as their sorrows. And I was aware of the joys continuing into my own time. At harvest festival the outsized marrows and sheaves of corn shared the font with marvellous ropes of wild rosehips, scarlet and shiny, strung together painstakingly by the Misses Sergeant and draped in several strands around the font like elaborate necklaces.

The church would have served a village three times the size of our meagre 400 souls. And thereby hung a tale. Observant people might notice the humps, bumps and ridges in the surrounding fields and they would be right in thinking that these were the ghostly remains of a much larger village swallowed up by the green grass. Other streets had been there once, where children played and cattle returned to the little homesteads at milking time. All gone! Was the Black Death responsible? Did the village never recover from the loss of more than half its men, women and children in the fourteenth century? On the north side of the churchyard, in the shadow of the tower, was an area quite without visible signs of burial. No ridges, no headstones. It was known as the Plague Pit and was a spooky place. When the wind moaned in the churchyard trees it sounded like the sobbing of grief and there was an old superstition that there was something rather dark and unmentionable about the north door. A friend of ours, whose mother died one winter when the south porch was blocked by snow, suggested to our village undertaker that the coffin should enter the church by the north door. 'I'll not have your mother go in by the north door,' he said flatly, and would not elaborate but dug out the snow-drift by hand.

The churchyard was a good levelling place. High or low, rich or poor, church or chapel, they all ended up there. Those were the days when everybody would have owned up to being a Christian of some sort, though internecine warfare was waged between the factions in our small community. As far as we were concerned it amounted to little more than raised eye-brows when the Wesleyans had a knock-about comic in a false red nose to sell the harvest festival produce from the chapel pulpit immediately after the service. But I remember (with my outrage still intact) when our vicar, speaking from the pulpit in veiled terms about the chapel people, said '. . . and it is left to us few Christians who remain to carry on the work of God.' It was as much as I could do to restrain myself from standing up in the pew and shouting, 'YOU CAN'T SAY THAT!'

Our family occupied the two front pews immediately under the pulpit. This had the disadvantage that we had to behave ourselves during the sermon and contrive to look as though we were listening when we weren't. Sermons went on interminably – thirty minutes was the norm – and we would start off listening because we knew Daddy would ask us afterwards what the text had been. But the vicar droned on and we would be miles away when there was a sudden change of tempo. From trailing away into smooth inaudibility he would suddenly, briskly, fortissimo, launch into 'And-now-to-God-the-Father-God-the-Son-and-God-the-Holy-Ghost-be-ascribed-all-honour-might-majesty-dominion-and-power' and the whole congregation would be galvanized into life, shuffling to their feet and rattling the small change in their pockets ready for the collection.

For a small country parish our church had a good choir, which was not altogether surprising as the excellent organist–choirmaster was also the headmaster of the village school; so it was a case of 'you and you and you volunteer'. Naughty boys were given the job of pumping the organ bellows and on the odd occasions when the boy ran out of muscle-power or concentration and the organ ground to a halt with a squeak and a groan it brightened things up no end.

It was in church that I experienced my first love affair. No, not with Philip, who sang in the choir and was very dishy, although I used to do my best to make eyes at him. No, it was with the *words*. The sheer blinding beauty of the words of the prayer book, and of the psalms in particular, gradually began to dawn on me and by the time I could read for myself they had enthralled me in wonder and delight. At first the meaning was quite unimportant. It was the richness of the sound and the prickling of the back of the neck which they created. 'What is man that thou art mindful of him?', 'If I take the wings of the morning', 'A day in thy courts is better than a thousand', 'Let my right hand forget her cunning' – the list is endless and I feel the prickling even now. One did not have to *understand* to realize that one was in the presence of inspired language. But as understanding came with the years a new dimension was added. 'Who can tell how oft he offendeth: O cleanse thou me from my secret faults' and 'He that sweareth unto his neighbour and disappointeth him not, though it were to his own hindrance . . .' Some things in life never change and are as relevant today as they were when King David found words to express them all those thousands of years ago. What a man he must have been!

While one could enjoy those sparkling word pictures about little hills skipping like young sheep, and being a door-keeper in the house of the Lord (with smart braided uniform and an array of silver buttons like the commissionaire at the Savoy Cinema) there were other bits of the service which were frankly baffling. What was to be made of 'Thou didst not abhor the Virgin's womb?' What on earth could it possibly mean? 'Virgin' presented no real problem; virgins were just unmarried ladies, weren't they? But 'abhor', that had a very worrying ring to it. And as for 'womb'! 'What's a womb?' I demanded of my mother and did not get a straight answer. It was, I gathered, a part of the body and we didn't talk about it. 'Is it only virgins who have them?' No, lots of people have them – and the subject was changed. But I brooded on it and wondered what would happen if I were to slip it into a polite conversation. Maybe next time Mrs Maw came to tea I would say casually, 'How's your womb today, Mrs Maw?' and see what happened.

As it was *very rude* to turn round and stare at the people behind us, we had to wait until the end of the service to see who had been in church. Many people had already been identified by their singing voices, for ours was a church where everyone sang lustily and many

Harvest festival

would sing in harmony. Farming families made up the greater part of the congregation, Daveys, Sergeants, Brocklesbys, Farrows, and at festival times they would opt themselves into the choir till there were more people in the choir-stalls than there were in the nave. Their anthems raised the roof and I longed for the day when I could join them.

There was another reason for wanting to see who was in church. It was a social convention that when newcomers moved into a village they could attend Communion at 8 a.m. without special significance, but when they first put in an appearance at Matins it was a sign that they were ready to receive callers. I remember my mother saying one day, 'The new people from Walk House were in church this morning. I must call.'

My mother usually visited people in the cottages on our return journey, especially the ones who were old, or sick, or lived alone, while we sat in the car and passed the time playing cat's cradle with a piece of string Daddy always seemed able to produce from his pocket.

The cottages stood in a row in the village street. There were no front doors, but a dark, echoing tunnel led to the back of the row where the doors opened on to a brick-paved yard, with a privy and a wash-house blocking the view of the narrow strip of garden beyond. Each cottage consisted of a tiny scullery and a single living-room looking on to the street. Here, behind the lace curtains, one could keep a sharp eye on the doings of the village. The cottages had no stairs but a ladder led the way through a square hatch in the ceiling into the bedroom above. The old ladies were wise enough not to attempt the ladder and slept in their living-rooms, which usually had an overpoweringly stale smell. Sometimes Pip and I accompanied Mummy on these visits, which we found rather embarrassing as we were talked about as though we were not there. But, having got over the embarrassment and accustomed ourselves to the smell, there was usually something interesting to look at – pot dogs, rose trellises on the wallpaper, biblical texts in Oxford frames and photos of menfolk in uniform.

The old ladies were mostly known as Grannie This and Grannie That and had a great deal to say, which was natural since they endured incredibly hard lives and seldom had anyone to talk to. My mother was a very good listener and was never highty-tighty or grand. So all the little worries of their lives used to come pouring out. After an outbreak of some rather nasty disease the well which supplied the cottages with water was condemned and sealed and a stand-pipe of mains water installed outside every back door. One might have thought this would be a welcome improvement, but the consensus of opinion was 'Noo! Watter do-ant taste of owt.'

Grannie Bolton had been three times married and was still, in her eighties, a formidable woman of ample proportions with a robust sense of humour. Her preference had obviously been for her first husband, Fred, and she let it be generally known that she wanted 'to be laid along mi first'. To this end she had bought the plot next to Fred's grave and every time a funeral was in the offing she would sprint up to the churchyard and put a posy of flowers on her plot in case somebody else inadvertently bagged it. On one occasion, so she told my mother at great length, the bell was tolling but she had no idea for whom.

'So I went to Grannie Russell and said "Oose di-ed?" and she didn't know. Well, I wasn't satisfied so I went to old Mrs Selby and I said

"Oose di-ed?"' – and so on up the row. But nobody knew. So up she scuttled to the churchyard, where she found the plot so overgrown with weeds that it required a hand-hook. She was busily engaged in slashing at 'all them 'emmylock and nettles when I slipped and got farwelted between two graves. I laughed that much I pee'd mi-sen,' she concluded, wiping her eyes at the thought of it.

When Grannie Russell died my mother commiserated with Grannie Bolton on the loss of a neighbour. Her response was not quite what my mother expected. 'Oh, it were time she went. That shed up yard were in a right pickle.'

There was something proper and respectable about dying in one's own bed. The alternative, fear of which hovered most unpleasantly over many old people, was the workhouse. I suppose our nearest workhouse, eight miles away, was not the worst that could be imagined. Nevertheless the great, nagging, haunting fear was two-fold: firstly, of being dug out from everything that was familiar – home, belongings, neighbours – and dumped in a strange environment where one became a non-person; and, secondly, of the disgrace – that one had failed to lay by enough for old age and that there was no family to call upon in the hour of need. To spend those last declining years in the 'wuckus' was an admission of failure on all counts. The word was spoken in low tones and jokes about the 'wuckus' were in bad taste. There, but for the grace of God . . . .

As autumn approached walking home across the fields acquired an exciting new prospect and we would arrive triumphantly with Daddy's hat full of mushrooms. There can hardly be a more pleasurable country pursuit than gathering the free gifts of nature, whether it be mushrooms, chestnuts, blackberries, or firewood, but there is something especially thrilling about spying those shining white caps half concealed in the grass. One of our little jokes was, 'Why are you never the second person to see a mushroom?' Answer, 'Because the first person who saw it picked it!'

On weekdays the main meal was dinner at eight – for the grown-ups, that is. The midday meal was called lunch. On Sundays dinner was always the midday meal and the evening meal was called supper. Sunday dinner was something akin to a religious ritual, not only in our house but in nearly every home in the land. And so it

Mushrooms in Daddy's hat

should be. Even the most primitive religions have at their heart a ceremonial meal where the whole family gathers together, hands washed, hair brushed, clothed in their Sunday best to enjoy a feast of thanksgiving presided over by the head of the house.

Our Sunday dinner seldom varied. We should have felt sadly deprived if it had consisted of anything other than roast beef and Yorkshire pudding, together with home-made horseradish sauce so hot that it prickled your nose and made your eyes run. Our joint was a 9 lb sirloin on the bone, with the fillet still *in situ*, beautifully rare and red. I remember Mummy once saying, 'I think we shall have to have a cheaper cut. This joint cost 11*s.* 6*d.*' It sounded like the end of the world. The nice thing about hot roast beef on Sunday was that it ensured cold roast beef on Monday (when the maids were busy with the laundry) and beef suet roly-poly on Tuesday – a great favourite.

The only change from beef was if Christmas Day fell on a Sunday, in which case it was turkey, or Easter Sunday when we had the first English lamb, as white as chicken meat, and mint sauce from mint brought on in the greenhouse. And from Christmas to Easter there was Christmas pudding every Sunday – the Sundays having been carefully counted by Cook and enough puddings made, though only the Christmas Day pudding came flaming and crackling to the table and had little silver charms in it.

Sunday afternoons were given over to leisure of a slightly more restricted order than on weekdays. We could go for walks but were not allowed to play with a ball, a hoop, or a skipping rope. We could play chess but not card-games (cards were associated with gambling), and we could read or sew. I think these were my father's rules; my mother would have had no such scruples.

It must have been about 1925 that we acquired our first wireless, a crystal set with headphones made by an enterprising and mechanically minded cousin. But it was soon superseded by a set with loud speaker to which we children were allowed to listen at teatime on Sundays. My memory recalls little but squeaks and wails ('oscillation' was a word I learnt from that era), and the all too regular playing of the National Anthem. At the sound of the first chord everybody had to rise and stand stiffly to attention for the duration. This included the dog. My father would point a purposeful finger at the creature and it would stand, motionless and apprehensive, ears and tail down, obviously wondering what it had done – only its eyebrows moving as it tried to see from which direction trouble might come.

Winter evenings were often rounded off by the whole family singing hymns round the piano, lit by candles and the glow of the fire. Tassie accompanied and had a pleasant soprano voice, while my mother sang contralto and my father bass. They slipped into harmony effortlessly and the richness and fulness of the sound was my introduction to part-singing which was to become such an important element in my later life. We took it in turns to choose our favourite hymns, always ending with 'The day thou gavest, Lord, is ended' – my father's favourite.

But sometimes the strain of being good and living life at an adult level for a whole day was just too much for us. Then bedtime came as something of a relief; once in the semi-darkness of the night nursery, with the small glow of the Kelly lamp through the open door and grown-ups safely out of earshot downstairs, we would give vent to our pent-up feelings, leaping up and down on our beds as though they were trampolines and inventing highly irreverent words to well-known hymn-tunes, attributing unlikely bodily functions to the Almighty and squealing with laughter at our own wit and audacity. This was quickly followed by moments of delicious terror, under the bedclothes, while we waited to be struck by lightning or some other form of divine retribution. But nothing happened: absolutely nothing. What an anti-climax! Was God more liberal than we gave Him credit for? Or worse, far worse, was He *not even listening*? What did one have to do to be really wicked?

Village Life

Village Life

Mary left to marry her Walter at about the same time as it became necessary for Pip and me to take school lessons a little more seriously. I had been sharing Honor's governess for some time, in a rather haphazard sort of way. I have no recollections of lessons as such but I well remember the pleasure and pride of being able to read, of doing sums, which were just like a wonderful game, and of forming individual letters and shapes in a double-lined exercise book – pothooks and suchlike which seemed more akin to the art of drawing. If I drew an 'S' which really pleased me I wanted to carry the book around all day and show it to everybody.

Then the day came when Honor started at a private school in Grimsby and her governess Margie Swallow sought pastures new. Margie was a remarkable young woman who, but for financial difficulties at home, would surely have gone to university and distinguished herself in the academic world. As it was, she joined my father's firm as personnel manager and eventually became a director. She lived with us at Thornton and the three of them, Daddy, Honor and Margie, went off to Grimsby together daily.

So a new governess had to be found for Pip and myself. She materialized in the form of Miss Sykes – Sykie as she was known – and life very definitely took an upward turn. Sykie was young, pretty, blonde and great fun. She was inventive and stimulating and a natural disciplinarian. Again, no memories of actual lessons remain but subjects such as geography, mathematics and nature study frequently became intertwined and were taught 'on the hoof', so to speak. We mapped and charted landmarks, studied different locations – a pond, a wood, an old quarry – to see what could be found there, brought things back in jam-pots and drew them, and learned to jump ditches with the aid of a stout pole. Suddenly, instead of sedate walks along the road to the village (in the hope of seeing Walter), we discovered the whole countryside and there was not a field, hedge, ditch, or tree that was not personally known to us.

In less clement weather there would be discoveries of other kinds to be made through books. Marvellous new horizons opened up with *Treasure Island*, *Little Women*, *Black Beauty*, *The Secret Garden* and *The Little Duke*, to be followed in time by the stories of Walter Scott, Kipling, Barrie, Masefield and yards and yards of epic poetry, much of which I can still recite.

Folk-songs we learnt too and we loved the strong, romantic stories of 'Barbara Allen' and 'Polly Oliver'. But our favourite was 'The Raggle-Taggle Gypsies-O', which lent itself particularly well to acting. I would be the lady in my high tower on top of the toy cupboard, yearning to join the imaginary gypsies dancing at my gate. Pip, my newly wedded lord, in an ostrich-plumed hat and mounted on her milk-white steed (the rocking horse) would ride frantically in search of me. But to no avail, for by this time I had joined the gypsies, kicked off my shoes and acquired a tambourine. It was a good story and our acting of it became quite polished, so that Daddy suggested we put a few items together and gave a little concert for the neighbours in our front hall to help raise money to buy a car for the district nurse. It was the first of many such efforts, for it was very much part of Daddy's philosophy that we should understand about money – how to earn it, how to save it, how to spend it wisely and how to give some of it away to good causes.

Sykie was strict about manners especially table-manners, and it went without saying that we had to eat everything put before us, like it or not. But once a week we were allowed to have a 'bad manners day' when we could eat pudding first and meat afterwards, eat with our fingers and with our mouths open, slurp our drink, snatch food without asking and disappear with it under the table. But before long nursery meals became a thing of the past and we graduated to the dining-room.

For the village children school was a rather different experience. The village school and school-house had been built by a wealthy and charitable lady in the 1870s. There was one playground for the boys and one for the girls (where never the twain should meet) and some primitive bucket-lavatories. The school consisted of a big hall with a stage at one end. The children ranged in age from four to fourteen and, while the infants occupied the stage, the two top classes shared the hall, sitting back to back. One class would be taught by the master, with blackboard and cane always at the ready, while the rest would be set to get on with copying or learning by heart on their own. The children all had a thorough grounding in the three Rs and the Bible and learnt to sing folk-songs, then being collected and revived with much enthusiasm. Despite the bleak conditions, the cold, the almost total lack of books and teaching aids, I guess there were not many children who left school unable to read, write and reckon.

Pleasures were very few. Nobody ever went away for a holiday and most children had to give a hand at home. But there always came a glorious day in the summer term when the whole school had an outing to Cleethorpes. The railway station was about a mile and a half from the school and transport was provided by local farmers. Three brightly painted, four-wheeled wagons, each drawn by a team of huge shire horses, picked the children up at the school, together with teachers, helpers and large hampers of food, and they would pass our house twenty minutes later on their way to catch the 8.30 train. We could hear them cheering from the moment they set off and as the cheering grew louder and louder we would race to the gate to watch them go by. What a sight it was! The farmers always took great pains to make the wagons and horses look their best. Manes were plaited with red, white and blue ribbons, horse brasses glistened and jingled, hooves were polished and the wagons decked with flags and bunting. The cheering never stopped, even on the occasions when it rained; one would have thought they'd have grown hoarse by the time they reached the station – but no! the whole process was repeated as they came home in the evening, tired out but oh, so happy!

For most country people life was a humdrum affair and what pleasures there were had to be home-made. Enterprising youngsters might cycle to Barton for a visit to the pictures, or a dance, or the annual fair, but once married with a family the women particularly were house-bound. So when, in 1922, my mother started a branch of the Women's Institute – an organization then in its infancy – it was an immediate success and was supported by women of all age-groups and

Children cheering all the way to the station

from all walks of life. They met in a disused chapel in the village and were soon engaged in a good deal more than jam and Jerusalem. In fact an average country-woman of the period was a competent cook and house-keeper with little need to learn new skills. It was in the realm of health, hygiene and child-care that the most significant improvements needed to be made. Old wives' tales died hard (particularly in relation to pregnancy and childbirth, sometimes with fatal results), and there was an acceptance that certain forms of illness or infestation in children were 'normal', and something they would grow out of. There was keen rivalry between young mothers who liked their babies to be fat but at the same time wanted them to walk before they were a year old. The result was often badly deformed bones. Another awful barbarity was that if babies didn't cut their teeth when it was thought they should, some mothers would lance the babies' gums with a darning needle. The appointment of a district nurse went a long way to improve matters and our nurse was a fairly regular visitor to WI meetings, where she could talk generally and nobody felt they were being got at.

Along with the aim of improvement went a lot of light-hearted enjoyment. A choir was formed to take part in the local music and drama festival and a drama group soon followed for the same purpose. The most unlikely people flung themselves into these activities with great gusto, but as far as drama was concerned the problem was the unsuitability of most one-act plays then generally available. The Alan Bennetts of this world had not yet arrived to bring ordinary folk to the stage and plays were written either for the class of person most likely to visit a theatre, or with some idea that it was good for the working classes to be socially uplifted. But to see our stout and solid farming wives playing duchesses and butlers was ludicrous. There was one lady who had great trouble with her 'aitches' and, after much coaxing and tuition, came out with the immortal line: 'Hobstinate you har' and hobstinate you halways will be to the hend of your days, and it's now that you're 'aving to pay for your hobstinacy.'

One of the highlights of the WI year was the annual meeting at the Albert Hall in London and attendance required considerable courage from a delegate who had probably never been further than Lincoln in her life. A roll-call, 'My longest journey', revealed many stay-at-homes, but a gasp of disbelief went up when a farmer's wife said, 'I don't know which is my longest journey, Moscow or Mexico – I've been to both.' Her father had been in the consular service. My mother encouraged some of the stay-at-homes to venture forth as delegates; she made all the arrangements for them and saw to it that they were accompanied on the journey, if she could not go herself. Mrs Welton, a farm manager's wife, was a spirited and comical lady and although the members did not get to hear much about the resolutions debated at the meeting, they simply fell about laughing at the round-by-round account of her visit to London. On making a close inspection of her hotel bedroom she had discovered a man's collar-stud under the bed and had not dared to take her clothes off in case the owner came back to look for it. Anyway, she assured her listeners, there wasn't a *proper* bed – only a mattress. This puzzled my mother until she realized that by a 'bed' Mrs Welton meant a feather-bed, which was what she had at home. The following morning Mrs Welton gave serious thought to breakfast and what would present the least hazard. 'So I settled for a boiled egg as I thought, well, a boiled egg's a boiled egg, ain't it, and there's not much they can do with that. But I could smell it coming up the stairs and I can tell you, ladies, that egg hadn't seen a hen for weeks.' So she abandoned breakfast and found her way to the Albert Hall by taking a short cut across 'them green fields' – Hyde Park.

There is no doubt that the WI brought a new quality into a great many lives in Thornton and was truly appreciated by its members. My mother found in it a new outlet for her talents and was much in demand throughout the county as a demonstrator of handicrafts. Somewhat to her surprise she also discovered a latent ability for organization which soon had her on the county executive and eventually led to the chairmanship of the Lindsey Federation, a post she held for thirteen years.

The WI brought many visitors to our house in the form of guest speakers and voluntary county organizers. They usually stayed for a meal, sometimes for the night. I remember one very smart and vivacious lady from London who wore a great deal of make-up and dark red nail varnish.. My father, who claimed to detest make-up, said she looked as if she'd got her fingers trapped in a door. He went on to add vehemently to my mother that he didn't know what he would do if she ever put muck like that on her face. What he did not know was that my mother, who had a very pale and colourless complexion, always discreetly used a little rouge on her cheeks. The next morning she came down to breakfast without it. Daddy looked at her uneasily.

'Are you all right, Helen?' he asked.

'Yes, thank you, dear.'

'Are you quite sure?'

'Yes, thank you, dear. Why?'

'You don't look very well.'

Her point having been subtly made, next morning she quietly went back to her rouge.

Meanwhile my mother's sister Tassie, not to be outdone, was off on a tack of her own. After a week's training course at Foxlease in Hampshire she came home, burning with her usual enthusiasm, and started a Girl Guide company. Tassie, who bore a striking resemblance to Lady Baden Powell, wore her uniform with considerable aplomb, cutting an impressive figure in cockaded hat and navy-blue serge suit generously bedecked with lanyard, whistle, badges and silver buttons. She was ably assisted by Margie Swallow in rather more modest attire and with quiet efficiency. Pip and I, of course, were too young to join the Guides but we hung hopefully around the edges whenever we had the chance and were sometimes allowed to make up numbers in the English country dancing. This was a summer activity on the lawn carried out with the aid of a portable gramophone and a pile of records. Oh, those lovely, lovely tunes! 'Selinger's Round', Rufty-Tufty', 'Haste to the Wedding' – what memories come flooding back!

There was also the summer camp in which our whole family participated in those first years, and I recall much ingenuity in cooking arrangements, with a clever oven made of a metal dolly-tub on its side let into a bank with a fire underneath and a stove-pipe up the back. And the never-to-be-forgotten latrines – wooden seats balanced precariously over a horrifying trench, shielded from public gaze by hessian screens, a bunch of green twigs tied with string to indicate if anyone was in there or not (twigs outside for 'vacant', twigs inside for 'engaged'; or was it the other way round? I never could remember).

For the rest of the summer Pip and I could think of nothing but camping. An old car rug and a few bean poles served as a tent in the orchard and, with the aid of Tassie's lanyard and whistle, our camp was run with military precision – tent inspection and drill, the line only being drawn at latrines. But our greatest enthusiasm was reserved for the camp fire. Sykie undertook the supervision of the fire while we foraged for sticks in the wood, which, thanks to the rooks above, were always plentiful. As the fire began to die down the really serious business of making dampers began. No one who has not made dampers on a camp fire can fully appreciate the call of the wild. First, straight ash twigs must be found and the bark whittled off one end. Next, a piece of dough (a simple scone mix) is pulled out and wrapped round the stick. Then the damper is turned slowly over the hot embers until it will slide off the stick. And, finally, the hole is plugged with a nice dob of butter and the delectable confection eaten while it is still hot, with the butter dripping through messily. Burnt bits, with fire-ash still sticking to them, merely enhance the authenticity of the experience.

The peak of the social year was undoubtedly the vicarage garden fête, an event which saw the village at its very best. Everybody gave a hand and our kind elderly vicar and his amusing wife endeavoured, somewhat against the odds, to direct the operation. But since he seldom managed to finish a sentence it was quite hard to understand what he meant, while the two of them would bicker amicably over endless misunderstandings.

'My dear, I do know what I'm talking about. In the orchard!'

'No, no, no, that's no good at all. We'll have it in the scullery where we always have it.'

'The scullery? You're talking through your hat – *it wouldn't even go in.*'

'What nonsense! It's always gone in before.'

And so on till after ten minutes it was discovered that one was talking about the hoop-la table and the other about the paraffin stove for the tea.

The fête had to be opened in a formal manner by a VIP – Lady Somebody or a bishop maybe. At the appointed hour the ringing of a large handbell (borrowed from the school) summoned everybody to the front of the vicarage where they were addressed in lengthy and worthy speeches and the fête declared open. It seemed interminable to us children, clutching our pennies in hot, sticky hands and longing to be first at the bran tub.

The sun always shone and there was something for everyone – side-shows, competitions, displays, teas, tennis tournament, fortune-telling and ice-cream. Nowadays children seem to eat ice-cream nearly every day but then it was the greatest treat imaginable, a once-a-year event. The ice-cream stall was under a beautiful weeping ash tree which formed a shady sort of tent. The ice-cream, which was locally made, was frozen custard of an amazing yellow colour and was scooped out of big metal drums and plopped into cornets. It was deliciously sweet and vanillary and we made it last as long as possible, pushing it down into the cornert with our tongues as we nibbled our way round the edges. Hygiene was not much in evidence and the delicacy probably contained high concentrations of brucellosis, bovine tuberculosis, listeria, salmonella and all the evils known and unknown to the medical profession. Fortunately, those were the days when most of us had our antibodies still intact and we survived, blissfully unaware of the risks we might be running.

Of all the side-shows, bowling for the pig was the main attraction. There, in a crate of staw, was a real live pigling, some two months old and given by one of our farmers. Though everybody would have a go during the afternoon it was not until early evening that the really serious bowling began. By that time the young farm-labouring lads had finished the afternoon's milking and would crowd in to play each other for this coveted little creature. There were six croquet balls and a large board with a hole so small that the balls could only just go through it. You stood behind the white line and rolled the balls along the ground. Whoever got the most balls through the hole won the pig and there was often an exciting play-off at the end. But the game took on a new dimension when it was discovered that our housemaid, Queenie, was a deadly accurate bowler. Queenie was a beautiful girl, so shy and modest that she could hardly lift her dark eyes off the ground. How her talent was discovered I don't know, but soon the young men were queuing up to pay for Queenie to win them a pig. They would take her to the fêtes around the neighbouring villages and in one season she won four pigs.

If there was one sure way to stir up strife at a village fête it was to have a baby-show, and such was the ill-feeling this event caused that it had to be dropped. Mothers turned their babies out smartly – new bonnets and bootees knitted by grannie and new dummy with ribbon – pink for a girl, blue for a boy. Fat babies were considered 'bonny' and the more folds and rolls of fat on their little arms and legs the better. The trouble came to a head when the matron of the local general hospital was asked to be the judge. Matron Brewer was a splendid down-to-earth lady who had been known to reduce doctors to tears. Imagine the reaction of a dozen proud mums when she described the fat as flab, removed the dummies to examine the babies' mouths for thrush and insisted on inspecting their bottoms for nappy-rash. It all ended in tears and the vicar's wife had to use all her tact and diplomacy to soothe ruffled feathers and restore some sort of calm to deeply hurt feelings. There were no more baby-shows.

The displays varied from year to year but the memory I treasure most is of one put on by an enterprising young woman from the next village who ran a children's ballet class. Eight diminutive and oddly assorted swans in white tutus and feathered head-dresses pranced and preened on a sort of wooden raft not much bigger than our kitchen table, which had been placed on the long orchard grass, while their teacher tottered on her points in their midst then died rather unconvincingly. I was totally absorbed and felt there was still a chance of saving her so long as her chest continued to heave up and down. Why didn't someone rush to her rescue? But the enchantment was rudely shattered by the conversation of two teenagers standing next to me. One said, 'Clever, init?' and her friend curled her lip and answered knowingly, 'Oh, it's the shoes you know. Anyone can do it if they have the shoes.'

All the ingredients of the village fête so far described were truly home-spun. The tennis tournament, on the other hand, introduced an imported and up-market element, attracting players from a wide area of North Lincolnshire. It was an American tournament for mixed doubles in which everybody played everybody and several tennis courts were pressed into service; three could be raised in Thornton and another two in Wootton, which necessitated a good deal of dashing about between courts in open cars, long scarves flying glamorously. The girls dressed up to the minute in short straight white dresses with the waist-line a good ten inches lower than where the waist-line was intended to be. Bobbed hair and a bandeau crowned the modern look which was set off by an almost obligatory cigarette smoked in a long holder. Nevertheless, this was more than a flappers' fashion show and some serious tennis was played. These tournaments could become a stepping-stone to playing for the county and many would-be champions were to be found doing the rounds.

In between the high days and holidays village life went on its quiet way with remarkable consistency. But it was never dull. What affected one affected all and a new baby was everyone's delight – though the whole village would know to the day how long after the wedding it was born. Before the days of cars and public transport the village shops were hotbeds of local gossip, none more so than the post office. Everybody had to visit the post office because it sold everything. In that tiny space with its worn brick floor and a counter either side you could buy postal orders and stamps, sewing cotton and buckets. Liquorice Allsorts and socks. As the shelf-space was strictly limited, dozens of items hung from the low ceiling so that you had to duck with every step. Standing as it did at the centre of the village, the post office enjoyed a commanding view up and down the street, across to the other shops, the church and the pub, so that no one could move without being closely observed by the postmistress, who liked to give a running commentary on what she saw and to put her own construction on events.

Postcards were fair game. 'I see Miss Robertson's having bad weather for her holiday,' she volunteered one day as she handed the card over. The arrival of the telephone provided her with another useful ear. But the vicar used to cycle the half mile to make his calls from our telephone (the only other one in the village), because, he said with scarcely concealed indignation, the post office used to *charge him*. On one occasion the husband in the cottage adjoining the post office was taken ill and the doctor had to be sent for by telephone. After his visit the doctor called in to thank the postmistress for her prompt action. 'What do you reckon to Smiley, doctor?' she asked. Not wishing to discuss the case with her the doctor shook his head. 'I knew what *that* meant,' she told my mother, 'so I wired for his relations.' The relations were none too pleased, on arriving post-haste from Doncaster, to find Smiley wheezing a bit but otherwise recovered.

Another rumour started that the widow in the cottage opposite was running an immoral house. That is hard to believe given that Mrs D was middle-aged with thin, grey wispy hair and thick pebble glasses that required a facial expression resembling a snarl to keep them up on her nose. Nevertheless, a row broke out between her and her next-door neighbour, who used to shout abuse and throw her washing-up water (and worse) across Mrs D's back yard. The widow took her complaint to the vicar and suggested that if he came to her house at a certain hour he would see for himself what she had to put up with. Foolishly the vicar allowed himself to be drawn into this little plot, and on trying to creep quietly up the dark passageway between the houses he fell over a bicycle with a great clatter. Out popped the neighbour and shouted, 'It's no use you going in there, she's got one with her already and she can't do with more than one at once.' The vicar fled.

But that was village life and it is just as true that had Mrs D's house caught fire everyone would have rallied round to help. She was, after all, 'one of us'.

The Singing Ploughboy

The Singing Ploughboy

It has never ceased to astonish me that farm labouring could be termed unskilled work. Few occupations call upon such a wide array of practical skills and this was particularly true in the days before the invention of sophisticated farm machinery. Nowadays much of the toil and, more significantly perhaps, much of the risk has been removed from farming by the combine harvester and the milking machine, the grain-drier and refrigeration. But I look back to the countryside of the 1920s where good husbandry was everywhere in evidence. Laying a hedge, ploughing a straight furrow with a team of horses, constructing and thatching a corn stack ('thacking' it was called in Lincolnshire) – these were skills in which men took great pride.

Although tractors began to appear on the land during the First World War, when there was a shortage of men, they did not really catch on until the Second World War. This was partly because farming itself became deeply depressed during the 1920s and '30s. Labour was cheap and plentiful, tractors required more capital outlay than most farmers could afford and there was a deep attachment to the old way of life which everyone understood and to which farms were geared. Those gentle giants, the shire horses, were the pride of the farming world and you couldn't turn wagoners into mechanics overnight.

There was not much choice for young lads leaving school in our part of the world – any more than there was for their sisters. There were a few apprenticeships in the usual trades, carpentry and so on, but in most families it was important for a lad to start earning immediately and, as his father was probably on the land, it seemed natural and inevitable that the son should follow suit.

Working clothes were almost standard. Brown corduroy trousers were worn, tied just below the knee with string. Boots were of leather, hob-nailed and steel toe-capped. The usual defence against cold was an army great-coat, a relic of the war readily available second-hand, and extra warmth could be gained by tying a piece of string round the waist. There was a saying that a piece of string was as good as an extra coat. In wet weather many men wore a sack, opened up along one seam, like a pointed hood over the head and pulled round the shoulders, giving them an oddly monkish appearance. Together with long hours and poor pay, the prospects did not seem all that attractive and mothers were anxious to discourage their daughters from marrying farm labourers because it sentenced them to a life of toil and hardship. But, as with the girls in service in the big houses, the large Lincolnshire farms provided these youths with a career structure; to become head wagoner or gaffman (head milkman) or foreman was to have some social status in the village, if not affluence.

Sometimes it was important for the lads to find a job where they could live in as there was no room for them at home. Our housemaid, Ivy, was one of nine children in an estate lodge cottage with one bedroom. There was never any question of them all being home together, so Ivy's brothers lived in on the farms where they worked, while the younger members of the family all shared a bed in their parents' room.

The lad leaving school to go on the land knew what he was letting himself in for. From his earliest recollections he had been on the fringe of farming, feeding animals, accompanying parents to hayfield or harvest and earning a few bob potato-picking during the school autumn holiday, which was granted especially for that purpose. At fourteen years of age a lad had neither the size nor the strength required for much of the work and he would have to be content for the time being to be given the dirty jobs and to put up with a good deal of horse-play and practical joking. There was always keen competition between the lads: who could lift the heaviest sack and hoist it on to his shoulders, who could do the most in the least time. But above all he longed for that great day – that landmark of growing up – when he took charge of a pair of horses and ploughed his first furrow.

My sister Pip had a childhood regret that she was not born a boy. She thought boys had more fun and she wanted to be a farmer, working with animals, especially horses. She always begged to have

The singing ploughboy

her straight hair cropped short like a boy and her favourite garment was a pair of shorts with an elasticized belt with a snake fastener. Whenever escape was possible she was off across the fields to Frogmore Farm where she soon learnt to catch the pony in the field, ride it bareback to the farm and harness it to the milk float. But her greatest achievement was to plough her first furrow at the age of ten, with two horses in hand, in the field immediately opposite our front gate. Of course, there was a good deal of assistance from a patient and slightly amused farm labourer, who lent his weight to the shafts when necessary and guided the plough on the tricky turn at the headland when it was all too easy to tip it on to its side. But she grasped the principles and learnt the commands which the horses obeyed so intelligently and came home radiating a sense of triumph. Every ploughboy must have felt the same.

The countryside was a quiet and peaceful place by today's standards and ploughing was a leisurely pursuit, carried out at a pace horses and men could keep up hour after hour, all day long. One might think it was a lonely job, but most young men would say it was one of the things they liked doing best. To be in charge of a team was like owning a little private kingdom where the smell of the horses, the clink and squeak of their harness and the larks in the sky were theirs for the working day. Behind them a large following of gulls and other birds worked the open furrow over thoroughly, cleansing the land of wireworms and leather-jackets and all the time in the world to do it.

How these lads used to whistle and sing! There wasn't anywhere else where you could let off steam like that and with the whole field to yourself you could make marvellous discoveries about vocal powers you didn't even know you had. On a still winter's day, with a nip of frost in the air, the sound carried over a wide distance and the countryside rang with the latest songs from film or review, hymns, old favourites from the war, folk-songs, even singing-games remembered from the playground. It was a lovely sound and I for one am glad that I can remember the singing, whistling ploughboy who was so special a feature of the farming scene.

Nowadays harvesting seems to be just another job. In the morning a field of standing corn, by teatime the straw baled, the corn in sacks, all done by one man and a machine. No excitement, no total involvement of the whole family and little sense of relief or achievement. But before the advent of the combine harvester and the grain-drier, harvest was a nerve-racking business, rightly regarded as the pinnacle of the farming year. Families were brought together in a super-human effort to beat the elements. There was a part for everyone to play – women, children, even the dogs. While the weather held, meals were brought to the fields and work went on until it was too dark to see.

The corn was cut by binder, a complicated piece of machinery that bound the corn into sheaves tied with string and threw them out, where they were picked up by the labourers and propped together in pairs to form stooks – eight or ten sheaves to a stook. Reaping started with the machine working round the perimeter of the field. As the square of standing corn grew smaller and smaller the rabbits were driven together in the middle until the moment came when they had to make a run for it. Bedlam would ensue as the boys, wielding sticks and aided by eager dogs, gave chase and what with the shouting and the barking and the general pandemonium, not many rabbits escaped and that week's frugal diet would be supplemented by rabbit pie.

If the weather was kind, the stooks stood in the field to dry for a few days and then the task of leading them to the stackyard began. There was a great art in loading the wagon to its maximum capacity and in building the stack correctly, and the work had to be done at top speed to release the wagon for its return to the field for another load. Finally, at a later date when there was more time, the stack was thatched with straw pegged down with string, to keep the rain out until such time as the threshing machine made its annual call. It was a fine sight to see half a dozen well-made stacks gleaming golden yellow in the autumn sunshine.

After the corn was gathered in many farmers allowed the wives of their labourers to glean the fields; in other words, any corn which had escaped the machine could be picked up by hand and used to feed the chickens which most cottagers kept. It was a very special scene, to watch the women in the fields filling their aprons in this way, and it seemed to me that little had changed since the biblical times of Ruth and Naomi.

Harvesting remains in my mind as a sort of country idyll, as if the sun always shone and the yield was always good. But there were times – disastrous times – when the rain poured down relentlessly and stooks stood in the fields till Christmas, blackened and sprouting. Then farmers were poor and hearts were sad.

There were others anxious to glean the last remaining grain from the stubble. Late in September the first of the pink-footed geese returned from their breeding grounds in Iceland to winter on the Humber estuary and the surrounding farmland. The first unforgettable sound of their distant honking was enough to send us dashing to the window, excitedly unlatching and folding back the shutters so that we could lean out to catch sight of the thin dark line in the sky that heralded their arrival. I can think of no more thrilling moment of my childhood, and no more evocative shout than 'The geese are back!' Soon the air was filled with their wild clamour as skein after skein, in chevron formation, flew over until many thousands darkened the sky. All through October their numbers grew. By night they roosted on the mud-flats of the estuary and on Read's Island. At first light they were off to seek feeding grounds further inland and would spend the day in stubble fields over a radius of many miles, returning to the Humber as light began to fade. They were with us till March and the sky seemed empty without them.

The corn harvest was only the beginning of a busy autumn. Lincolnshire farms produced vast acres of potatoes which, after lifting by great armies of school children, were stored in long graves or clamps. A straw base was laid in these and the potatoes heaped up to form a ridge along their length. Then they were covered with straw and a drainage pit dug round the edge, the earth being thrown up on to the straw to keep the light out; little straw 'chimneys' were left along the ridge to provide ventilation. Sugar beet was a new crop which claimed more acres all the time. It was heartily disliked by the

'The geese are back!'

men who had to handle it because the beet had to be lifted, topped and tailed entirely by hand at the very worst time of year – November.

One of the most beautiful skills practised in the countryside was the making of farm carts and wagons. The four-wheeled, double-shafted wagon can surely be described as the Rolls Royce of the farming world, and we were fortunate to have in Thornton a craftsman of exceptional ability. Jack the Joiner (carpenter and undertaker) had his workshop at the approach to the main village street. It consisted of a series of open-fronted sheds under a long pantiled roof, with plenty of waste space alongside to store piles of timber and farm machinery awaiting repair. It was a busy place, ringing with the sound of saw and hammer, the shop-floor always ankle deep in curly wood shavings that smelt sweetly of resin. With power tools not yet invented the skills of the carpenter and the tools he used would have been easily recognized by his Roman counterpart, for the saw, the plane, the adze and the hammer had scarcely changed in two thousand years. I suppose Joseph's carpenter's shop in Nazareth would have looked pretty much like Jack's and would have smelt the same.

Though we children were not allowed to go near enough to be a nuisance or to get into danger, there was much to be seen from the gate and there was one process in the making of a wagon that was not to be missed. The most intricate job of the whole procedure was the construction of the wheels. Wheels required three different kinds of native hardwood – the hub was of English elm, the spokes of oak and the rim of ash, because ash can be persuaded to bend into a curve. But it was what happened after that that was really exciting. The wheel had to be shod with an iron rim and for this it was rolled across the street to Frank the Blacksmith's forge, which was conveniently situated opposite Jack's workshop.

These two men shared a lot of work and I can see them now in my mind: Jack, a big man, stolid and quiet, with his flat cap and his special flat pencil behind his ear; Frank, wiry and dark, with a quick-silver nature and a ready smile, always wearing the leather apron which played so important a role when he cradled the hoof of a horse during shoeing. The smithy was a shambling building in two parts, the first an open-fronted shed where horses were shod, the second an inner room, quite dark, where the forge fire and the anvil were located. The great bellows would send the fire from a dull glow to a roaring blaze in a few seconds, lighting up the faces of the men at work.

It was this fire which heated up the special tall thin cupboard that opened outwards into the yard and in which the iron rim for the wheel was heated to white hot. While this was taking place the wheel itself was got ready, being placed on a round platform floating in a sort of bricked-edged well, and secured with a block through the hub. Then came the big moment as the rim was quickly rolled out of its cupboard by Frank and his assistant with long-handled tongs and flung over the wheel that almost immediately burst into flames. The men started to hammer the rim down over the wheel with all speed but soon were forced to release the lever that plunged the whole platform with a splosh into the well. There was a great hissing and a huge cloud of steam that enveloped everybody for a second or two, then up came the wheel again and the hammering continued. More flames; down went the wheel; more hissing (this time slightly more subdued); then up again for a final beating into place. As the iron rim cooled so it shrank on to the wood. Altogether it was a spectacular operation in which speed and accuracy were the essential ingredients.

Finally, the wagons were painted in bright colours, sometimes blue or green but more often orange, and they were finished off with lines and intricate scrolls and whirligigs and the name of the farmer and the farm. A wagon in all its glory was a work of art good enough to be exhibited in an art gallery.

Round about the month of November a very important event would completely take over the housewife, her routine, her time and her energy. It went by the name of 'putting the pig away'. 'Well, I shan't be able to come next week. I shall be putting the pig away.' The phrase never varied and was a thoroughly understood reason why nobody could be expected to put their mind to anything else.

The procedure involved the farmer's wife and the labourer's wife alike. A brick pig-sty was to be found at the bottom of most cottage gardens and it was quite usual for a farmer to give each of his labourers a pigling in the spring, or at any rate to let them buy one cheaply. They were reared on skimmed milk and meal, household scraps, potato peelings, apples and garden vegetable waste. This was the great advantage of the pig: it ate anything and everything and was thus cheap to rear. By November it was ready.

Lincolnshire people liked their pigs to be fat and 20 score (400 lbs) was not unusual. There was a lot of friendly rivalry among pig owners and time would be spent leaning on the pig-sty gate, silently appraising the pig and assessing its likely weight. As Mrs Bratby said to Mary one day, 'I never did go much on dogs and cats, but I can take to a nice pig.' But whether you took to it or not, the fateful day would arrive when three or four men banded together to help each other and the air was full of terrible squealing as the wretched pig had its throat cut in cold blood. Even our own two pigs, who rejoiced in the names of Lambert Simnel and Perkin Warbeck, met this fate one year, down by the stables. Though we were kept well away at the time, afterwards we felt compelled to visit the place of slaughter, skin prickling in horror and eyes peeled to catch sight of the merest splash of blood remaining on the walls.

It has been said that you can eat every part of the pig except its squeal and that is not far short of the truth. For three or four frantic days the housewife 'put the pig away'. That meant preserving the meat by various means to provide food for the months to come. Ham and bacon, chine and brawn, blood-puddings and mincemeat, sausages and lard: it was a mammoth task. Sometimes ham or sides of bacon could be hung in the chimney to smoke, but more often they were salted in brine. Chine was stuffed with vast quantities of chopped parsley; brawn was made from the pig's head, including cheeks, tongue, brains, ears and snout, set in a solid jelly made from the trotters. Any little bits and scraps were placed on one side, put through a large mincer screwed to the kitchen table, and mixed with bread-crumbs, salt, pepper, spices and sage to make sausages. The sausage skins were prepared by cleaning the pig's gut with the back of a wooden spoon and great skill and care were needed to avoid making holes in the skin which was then threaded on to a plain pipe on the mincer for filling. Deft hands twisted the long rope into individual sausages. In those days, too, it was still the custom to put real meat into the 'mincemeat', as was the original intention, for the fruit, sugar and spice helped to preserve the meat for many months. And every scrap of fat was rendered down in a huge pan for lard. Nothing was wasted. If one were to call at a farmhouse during this busy time the farmer's wife would probably say, 'Come in, ducky, and sit down.' But there would be nowhere to sit. Trotters on this chair, a basin of lard on that, every available space earning its keep and never a moment to lose.

There was a well-observed custom known as 'Pig Cheer'. A small collection of choice bits and pieces, like a mixed grill, was put together in the pig's caul – a net-like skin covering the stomach – and taken round to friends and neighbours, who would take the goodies out and return the caul to be refilled for the next one. There was much running to and fro and much cheerful goodwill and satisfaction at a job well done. And when the neighbours killed their pig they would do the same for you.

Spring brought another memorable landmark in the life of the countryside. 'Flitting Day' might not appear in the calendar alongside saints' days and public holidays, but anyone could have told you that it was 5 April. That was the day farm labourers changed their jobs. While many would stay on one farm for many years others would move from farm to farm, never staying very long in one place. Sometimes it was to better themselves, or maybe they didn't see eye to eye with their boss, or they just fancied a change. And Flitting Day was the only day they could do it. I often heard our maids say, 'We're flitting.' It simply meant, 'Dad's changed his job and we're moving house.' It was perfectly respectable and not to be confused with 'doing a moonlight flit.'

As the cottages were tied to the farms the house went with the job and in that sense accommodation was never a problem. The custom was that the farmer whose employment you were entering provided you with a cart and horse to carry you and all your possessions to the new location – seldom more than five or six miles away. All day long on Flitting Day the roads carried this unusual traffic and a strange sight it was. The cart was loaded high with furniture, the iron bedstead and bedding, a crate of chickens, a bicycle, the mangle, and always odd things hanging out at the back – often the broom with a bucket swinging squeakily on it, because they were the last things in use before the final 'goodbye' to the place that had been home. On the front of the cart sat the family, perched on their belongings, clutching the cat, the children bewildered, the wife apprehensive about what she might find at the other end, for all the world like refugees.

There was a fierce pride among the women that they had left their cottages spick and span for the new tenants, and always indignant stories about how they had scrubbed their way out backwards and left a garden with blackcurrant bushes and gooseberries, only to come to a dirty cottage with a garden that was nothing but a bed of nettles. The tied cottage system came in for a lot of abuse but before the days of

Flitting Day

council houses it had many advantages. The rent was low. Half a crown a week was the norm, deducted from the weekly basic wage of 26 shillings. And the cottage usually offered a large vegetable garden, chicken run and pig-sty, and many necessities came cheaply from the farm – milk, potatoes, straw for bedding the animals, and the pigling aforementioned. Not that facilities were anywhere near standard. The cottages where the Bratbys lived were decidedly substandard. There was no water supply and the menfolk from the three cottages lugged a large tank on wheels up to the tap in our stable yard before going to work in the morning and again after returning from work in the evening. As there was no form of drainage the washing-up water used to be slung straight out of the doors, across the brick path, on to the earth bank which was thick with slime and a regular scavenging place for rats.

'Flitting' meant that part, at any rate, of the rural population could not truly be said to belong to any one village. One might have been born in Limber, schooled in Barrow, married in Thornton, and so on. Yet I suppose it affected a small proportion of labouring families and there were others whose forebears had stayed put for generations. There was a class of true locals who had irregular jobs around the edges of farming, yet were indispensable to it. They were their own bosses and appeared to work only when it suited them and their sometimes dubious existences were regarded with tolerant amusement.

One such was old Bunnyhares. I never knew what his real name was. Bunnyhares was what everybody called him. An elderly man, shabbily dressed, he was still tall and erect. He lived in a cottage behind the pub – well, more of a shed it was really – and seldom spoke to anyone. He was a rabbit catcher and used to push an old iron bicycle around the place with pairs of dead rabbits tied by the back legs hanging from the handle-bars and crossbar. Farmers employed him to clear their land where rabbit holes were known to contain breeding colonies. He had a variety of ways of dealing with rabbits – traps, nets, ferrets – but the most ingenious and skilful method required the use of a long bramble spray. This technique was for use when there were young in the burrow and it was not safe to send ferrets down for fear of losing them. Bunnyhares took his time to select the right bramble. It must be very long, strong and whippy, with plenty of large thorns and no side-shoots. Then he would prepare it, removing enough thorns at the thick end to make a comfortable handle. He had already discovered, by lying on the ground and listening closely for some minutes, exactly how far into the burrow the nest was. Then he would probe delicately with the bramble until he knew he had reached the nest and, by turning and screwing the bramble round slowly, he could feel when the thorns had successfully snagged the rabbit's fur. And out it came, the first of many. It was Bunnyhares' speciality.

We never witnessed this extraordinary feat, of course, but Daddy had been allowed to accompany him on one occasion. Bunnyhares had even let him have a go with the bramble but to no avail, his unskilled efforts earning him the comment, 'Aa niver se-ed owt so un'eppen.' The closest Pip and I came to rabbiting was to beg some salt from Cook to put on their tails. The Hilly Pits were full of rabbits and we loved nothing better than to go there, each clutching a little screwed-up piece of paper containing salt. 'If you put salt on their tails you'll catch them,' Cook used to say, and we believed her implicitly. But we soon tired of trying to creep up on the rabbits and spent the rest of the time roaring up and down the steep, grassy slopes that had once been a quarry.

Another highly skilled occupation which has now gone was droving. Drovers were oddly independent individuals who seemed to spend most of their time doing nothing, but who could walk 20 miles in a day when called upon to do so. Before the days of cattle transporters animals had to walk to and from market and every farmer knew where to find a reliable drover for the task. Thornton had two of them, the Burnetts, father and son. They were colourful characters, literally and metaphorically, being red-headed scallywags. Young Ginger had the reputation of being a skiver, but judging by the number of young red-heads in the school playground he evidently found sufficient energy for at least some activity. . . . And I well remember Ginger's broken ankle which caused much merriment in the village. Patients from Thornton had to go across the water to Hull for specialist treatment, and we used to see Ginger swinging along on his crutches on his way to the station, a roller-towel round his neck as a sling for his foot which was wrapped in a yellow duster. This went on for months, the joke being that the yellow duster, the sling and the crutches only came out once a fortnight for the trip to Hull where he collected his 'club' money.

However, when it came to droving the Burnetts had no equals. There was in our part of the world a network of back lanes with wide grass verges which were used as drove roads. They were not necessarily the shortest route from A to B, but they avoided the villages and had other advantages. All roads led to Brigg, a small town eight miles away, long famed for its cattle market and its annual fair. The Burnetts would set off at crack of dawn and pick up their assignment from the farm. With knapsacks on their backs and stout sticks in their hands they would make their leisurely way to market by way of Burnham and Race Lane. There was a little hollow with a few trees and a small pond at

Ginger

the side of the lane and this place went by the name of Noon Lairs. Here they rested, watered their animals and ate their packed lunch of bread and cheese. Then on to market where they delivered their charges to the appropriate quarter and then hung about to pick up a job for the return journey. They were well known by the local farmers who frequented the market and would present themselves at the right moment when they saw who was buying. Often their return journeys took them to other destinations, requiring a night away from home. But they had a rare native instinct for making do and sleeping rough.

One other odd character springs to mind. Albert's strange job had really gone before my life began, but I remember him as an old man, very small and made smaller still by his bandy legs, with a face as brown and wrinkled as a walnut. He wore an old broad-brimmed straw hat and a gold ear-ring in his left ear. (There was a superstition in our part of the world, and especially among seafaring folk, that piercing the ears improved the eyesight.) He was one of the last of the old marsh shepherds whose job it had been to herd sheep from inland farms to the coastal marshes for the summer, where the grazing was good and the salt was healthy for their feet. He and his dog would stay with them all summer long, living a solitary life in a wooden hut. Albert had been born in the 1840s and christened after the Prince Consort, as so many babies were then. He had never been to school and could neither read nor write. But he could count sheep and he did so in an ancient way, the origin of which is lost in the mists of time. With the aid of a notched stick he would count, 'Yan, tan, tethera, pithera, pin, slattera, lattera, covera, dovera, dick,' slide his thumb to the next notch and begin again – 'Yan, tan, . . .'

Marsh shepherding had disappeared by the early years of this century but in his old age Albert still gave a hand at lambing time if extra help was needed. In earlier times sheep had been big business in North Lincolnshire but, with claims that Australian wool was better and New Zealand lamb leaner and cheaper, the trade fell away till big herds became a rarity. Nevertheless, most farmers kept a few sheep and lambing time was a season that required special skills and long hours. In a climate that was sometimes hostile in the early months of the year, when the wind was fixed cruelly in the east for weeks on end, some form of shelter was important. Ewes and lambs were usually kept in the home paddock, close to the farmhouse, so that supervision was less demanding. Lambing pens were made of hurdles thatched with straw, arranged in a zig-zag formation and roofed over with more thatched hurdles. Well bedded with straw inside, these pens provided somewhere cosy for the animals to go out of the driving rain and snow, from whatever direction it might come.

There was always something fascinating about lambing time and nowhere better than the Hilly Pits to keep an eye on what was going

'Yan, tan, tethera . . .'

on. The Hilly Pits themselves provided natural shelter and grazing on land that was no good for anything else. There was no prettier sight than that of the lambs racing and chasing in their games up and down the grassy slopes. It was there also that Pip and I first saw a lamb wearing another lamb's skin and had it explained to us that the mother of the dead lamb would now accept the orphan lamb as her own, because of the smell of her own one's skin.

Despite the obvious welfare of most farm animals there was, I believe, a great deal of gratuitous cruelty. It was partly man's innate hunting instinct and partly a desire to hit back at a hard world. No cat or bird was safe from the young lads of the village, for whom torture and death was a way of wielding power. Birds'-nesting was a passion. In spring gangs of boys roamed the hedges with sticks, robbing nests of eggs and killing 'bubs'. Killing was sport.

Many children were brought up violently, both at home and at school. Near us there was a small-holding where the man was known for his fiendish temper; he used to beat his three young sons mercilessly. Sometimes, when we passed that house on our walks, we could hear the father shouting and the boys howling or groaning. It was a fearful place and we hated going past. The boys in turn had the reputation of being school bullies, especially the middle one who was a little monster. I experienced this at first hand on one occasion. I was by the low wall that separated the orchard from the road, looking at a robin's nest in the ivy, when the boy came along. He lunged at me in a threatening manner and I ran for my life, my heart in my throat nearly choking me. As I glanced back over my shoulder he was climbing over the wall into the orchard. When I plucked up courage to return, much later, the young robins had had their heads cut off. For days afterwards I was haunted by the sickening thought that my own curiosity about the robins had brought about their horrible end.

Cruelty came from the most surprising quarters. Our own gardener, Watson, a kind man in most respects, used to stamp on birds caught in the strawberry nets – mostly blackbirds and thrushes feeding young. Gardening did not go hand in hand with nature; nature was the enemy, consisting almost entirely of pests and weeds. I well remember another horrifying occasion when our butler, George, brought a mouse in a trap, still alive, into the kitchen and released it on to the hot plate of the range, where it ran half way round, shrieking as it burned, before falling into the fire. He laughed at my horror and Cook said, 'You shouldn't have done that in front of the children.' Doing it was all right – but not in front of the children.

Yet there were other aspects of cruelty which never entered our heads. Mummy had a crocodile dressing-case, wore lizard-skin shoes with handbag to match and had a hat decorated with a beautiful blue bird's wing. On her dressing-table were tortoise-shell hairbrushes, carved ivory trinket boxes and a silver jewel box whose lid was set with butterfly wings. They were part of everyday life, beautiful and expensive, to be admired and treasured. We never thought about where they came from or by what means they had been made for our delight.

Whether there was more cruelty then than now I'm not sure. Because cruelty is now frowned upon it has become more covert, though one knows that so-called 'sports' such as badger-baiting and dog-fighting still exist. And I rather suspect that the preoccupation of male birdwatchers and conservationists with birds of prey is a sort of voyeurism. Killing is still fun, whether you do it yourself or whether you get your thrills from seeing peregrine, eagle, or sparrowhawk do it for you. And whether factory-farming methods are more acceptable than the overt cruelty of old is a moot point; the fact that they are prompted more by greed and an indifference to suffering than by an actual blood-lust does not make them any more creditable.

Yet while the cruelty I so much deplored as a child was going on there were people who were already doing something to restore the balance. John Davey readily admitted that he too had been a savage in his youth, but in later years his farm became a haven for wildlife and men who worked for him were constantly encouraged, by his example and enthusiasm, to use a gentler approach. He planted spinneys in which redpolls nested and had a plantation of Christmas trees to provide both profit and habitat. And he championed the wild geese against persecution by wild-fowlers, taking the battle all the way to parliament. He was not the only man I knew who could spot a lark's nest in a hayfield he was mowing, stopping to plant a stick in the ground as a marker and giving it a wide berth with the mower.

By and large the countryside of the 1920s survived the depredations made upon it by men and young savages. Larks survived the mowing of the hayfields better than today's cutting of grass for sileage, which takes place at least a month earlier. Permanent grassland which had never seen a plough, much less weed-killer or fertilizer, produced a great range of wild plants and butterflies. I especially remember damp meadows covered with cowslips and orchids, dry pastures colourful with scabious, oxeye daisies, sorrel and clary and cornfields ablaze with scarlet poppies and supporting a large population of partridges, both native greys and 'Frenchmen'. The countryside seemed more accessible then. Children played in the fields and woods, building 'houses', collecting frog-spawn, picking blackberries and gathering firewood. In a sense it belonged to everyone.

Green and Pleasant Land

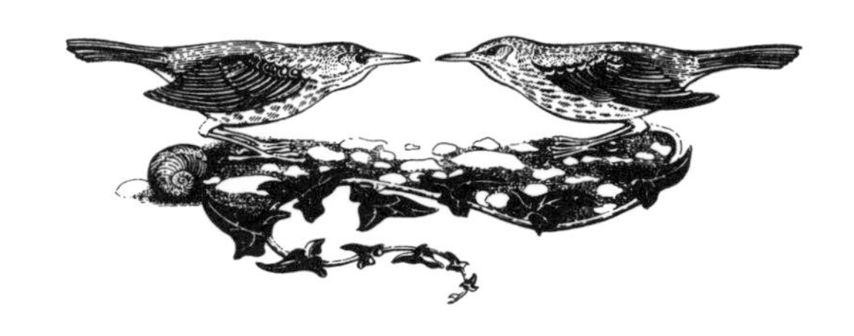

Green and Pleasant Land

I will not cease from mental fight,
Nor shall my sword sleep in my hand,
Till we have built Jerusalem
In England's green and pleasant land.

William Blake, a true countryman at heart, was not contemplating a Jerusalem of bricks and mortar. He lived during the Industrial Revolution and was appalled by the dark satanic mills and what he saw as the rape of our green and pleasant land. Jerusalem, to him, was a sort of ideal to which we could all aspire if we put our minds to it. More than that, it was an ideal that had to be fought for – that was worth fighting for – the mountains green, the pleasant pastures and the clouded hills. He saw it all so clearly yet, some two hundred years after Blake, here we are fighting his battles with renewed urgency.

Our corner of Lincolnshire was spared the satanic mills and my childhood was spent in a land without pesticides or chemical fertilizers, tractors or bull-dozers. Farmers went about their work in much the same way as they had since the Enclosure Acts wrought such enormous change in the countryside, obliterating most of what had gone before. There were still a few vestiges of the old order. The ridge and furrow showed where once farmers had cultivated their arable land in a communal system of strips, side by side with their neighbours; there is an area still called The Intake where a greedy landlord enclosed common land, robbing small farmers of their age-old grazing rights;

and an ancient farm, The Grange, was once probably the site of Thornton Abbey's great tithe barn.

For a generation after enclosure the landscape must have looked strangely naked as the countryside was denuded of trees and copses to make fencing for the new fields. But once the newly planted hedges began to grow nature re-established itself, as it always does if given half a chance. Coverts planted to provide the fox-hunting landowners with sport also became home to a wide variety of wildlife.

To me, as a child, it seemed as if hedgerow and pond, woodland and meadow were there for my delight. I was born with a sharp sense of observation and a persistent curiosity that drove most of my elders and betters to distraction. There were those who thought my continuous 'Why?' merely perverse; but I really did want to know, and learning to read and finding out how to make use of books was like learning to fly. Suddenly the whole world was there for the taking. Nowhere was my curiosity more acute than in the world of nature, especially of birds. While Tassie fired my enthusiasm and John Davey shared his great knowledge with me in a way that was neither pedantic nor patronizing, the seed of that yearning was already there and would not be denied.

The first bird to endear itself to me was the house martin, a large colony of which nested in the cornice above our nursery window. They would arrive in April and start patching up their old nests or starting new ones. From the window I could watch their every move at close quarters and long familiarity made them members of the family. To this day I find there is something very special about the quibbling noises they make among themselves, the 'chiz-it, chiz-it' alarm note at the sight of a hawk and the way the babies peep out of the small holes in the mud nests, looking like a row of little nuns in their navy-blue and white habits.

There were swallows in the cowsheds next door, and I knew them too, but they were neighbours, not family. My favourites were always the familiar birds in our own garden and I delighted in watching them and learning to recognize them individually. Blackbird and song thrush, robin and wren, hedge sparrow, finch and tits – I wanted to know all about them and to be able to tell them apart by their various calls, their silhouettes and flight, nests and eggs. This interest grew to a passion in the breeding season when the birds were at the peak of their plumage and song, and their behaviour was suddenly lively and purposeful.

Studying them and finding their nests was a lonely pursuit, almost secret, for few people could share the intensity of it. Only I knew how long I was prepared to stand, motionless and silent, watching a bird with a beakful of nesting material, waiting for it to lead me to its nesting site. Other people mostly found nests by accident, blundering about in the bushes and disturbing everything. There was no finesse in that and you learnt nothing about the birds.

As the yew hedges that Grandpa had planted began to grow they provided perfect places for blackbirds and song thrushes to nest. I noticed that blackbirds will return to the same nest for a second brood, maybe even a third. Thrushes like to start again and make a new nest, spending precious time when they could have been getting on with it. Blackbirds choose good sites and keep the nest tidy: thrushes sometimes choose sites that are too obvious or too exposed to the elements and they are apt to leave tell-tale streamers of building material. I remember one thrush that had a passion for flowers from the rockery so that the nest and hedge were decorated with aubrietia, white arabis and forget-me-nots. On another occasion a thrush's nest was wrecked and all the eggs but one broken. Knowing the eggs had been laid on the same day as those of a nearby blackbird, I transferred the unbroken egg to its nest and had the pleasure of seeing the blackbird bring up a family of four of its own and one thrush. All in all, blackbirds are much tougher in the survival game, which is why there are many more of them.

Sometimes there are other, more subtle ways of distinguishing birds. By chance, I found a nest too high up in the hedge for me to see and I enlisted John Davey's help. As we approached the hedge the bird slipped off and flew away on the far side. John stopped. 'I can tell you now it's a song thrush,' he said. 'Did you hear that drumming sound as she flew off? Only a song thrush does that.' I never forgot.

Birds' eggs were, to me, absolutely mesmeric and although I did not collect them, I wasn't beyond handling them in order to have a good look. Sometimes this resulted in accidents – a broken egg or a deserted nest because of too much interference. When that happened I suffered terrible pangs of remorse; on waking next morning it would be my first thought and my heart would sink like a stone to the bottom of my stomach. Nevertheless, I can understand the addiction of the ruthless egg-collector. Without a conscience, there's nothing inside him to check his obsession.

The huge variety in birds' eggs has always been a source of wonder to me – not only between one species and another but also between one egg and another of the same species. Obviously, most shapes and markings are for practical purposes. Ground-laying birds have pointed eggs so that they don't roll away, shore-birds lay eggs that look like stones, while birds that nest in holes usually have white eggs because camouflage is unnecessary. But that does not account for the marvellous scribbling marks on the yellow hammer's egg. And never two eggs identical! That goes way beyond practicalities.

Outside the garden lived other birds that gradually became great favourites. The whitethroat, with his harsh, jangling little song, danced above the road-side hedge and proclaimed that summer had really come. Whitethroats are not common now, as they used to be, and I never hear one without conjuring up in my mind the pink dog roses, white mayflowers and honeysuckle that grew in the hedges of my childhood. Another favourite, with us the year round, was the linnet – so drab a little finch for much of the time, but beautiful in the spring when he assumes a cocky rose-red cap with bib to match. There on the telegraph wire he would sing 'chic-a-dee, chic-a-dee', or fly off with a bounding flight uttering his 'tuc-a-tuc', a distinctive sound by which linnets can be identified at any season. Once so common in Lincolnshire and seen in large flocks in winter, linnets have suffered badly as a result of modern farming methods, for they rely on weed seeds in unploughed winter fields.

It was in a hedge sparrow's nest (we never knew it by the name dunnock) that I first saw a young cuckoo. Almost full grown, it was a repulsive sight, overflowing the tiny nest, puffing out its neck feathers into a grotesque sort of frill and opening that enormous red gape alarmingly. I was both shocked and fascinated.

The hedge sparrow was also responsible for a shock of quite another kind. My father was not a countryman born and bred and I suppose he hadn't had the advantage of my deeply rural start in life. He told me one day, as we walked home from church, that the hedge sparrow we had just seen on the road was the wife of Cock Robin. At the age of seven I knew perfectly well from my own observations that he was

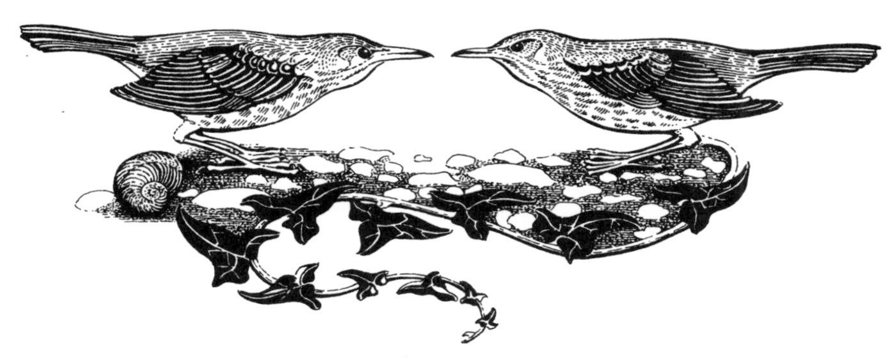

'Making long beaks'

wrong. Mr and Mrs Robin are alike and their eggs a mottled rusty colour; Mr and Mrs Hedge Sparrow are also alike, their eggs an exquisite sky blue. But never until that moment had it occurred to me that fathers could ever be wrong about anything. They knew everything there was to know and they were always right – weren't they? I was so taken aback that for a moment I didn't know how to handle the situation. It was the shattering of a basic belief and the destruction of a comfortable certainty, as if someone had just told me there was no Father Christmas. But as soon as I had recovered from the shock I began to argue with him and finally he conceded that he didn't really know and that maybe I was right. It was a great revelation to me and once I knew he was not invincible I plucked up courage to stand up to him more often. He had always been a great disciplinarian of the gun-dog variety (except on Sundays) and we were all a little in awe of him, as children were supposed to be of their fathers in those days. But I think he secretly admired my small defiance.

In species where the sexes are alike (robin, hedge sparrow and song thrush, for example), there always seems to be a lot of elaborate posturing in the breeding season, to establish the facts, as it were. Thrushes have a comical ritual which I called 'making long beaks'. Two males face each other, beaks almost touching, and elongate their bodies until beak, back and tail are more or less in a straight line. In that position they stay absolutely motionless for ages, each daring the other to be the first to move. And somewhere in the background there is a female, the bone of contention, pottering about and pretending not to be in the least bit interested in the outcome.

Two other birds were so much a part of the daily scene at Thornton that it is hard to realize that they are now both on the endangered species list. One was the tree sparrow and the other the barn owl. Tree sparrows lived in a mixed colony with the house sparrows in the ivy on the front of the house. It was a long time before I tumbled to the fact that they were not ordinary sparrows – birds so common that one took them for granted and didn't even bother to look at them properly. When I first noticed the pretty chestnut cap and the smart black-and-white bib I rushed to my bird book and was wildly excited with what I discovered. Then I began to listen to their calls which were so like, yet so unlike, their rather vulgar cousins'. Everything about the tree sparrow is refined. It is a charming little bird and identifying it by every means became such an obsession with me that it is locked into my head for ever and, although it is years since I saw or heard one in England, I know that the least sound would trigger the immediate response – 'Tree sparrow!'

The barn owls lived in the big chimney on the west wing of the house. Often we would see their pale, ghostly figures glide over the lawn and the shrubbery to alight on a favourite post of the field fence. At nesting time there was always a great commotion because young barn owls are very noisy. In the early days, when I was still sleeping in Tassie's room, I used to be able to watch them through the side window that looked out on to the chimney. At dusk they would emerge and sit on the edge of the chimney stack, huddling together and looking for all the world as if they had been badly hand-knitted. They would emit the most weird, blood-curdling noises, hissing, snoring and sometimes even sounds like deep breathing. I remember once a visitor slept in that room. She came rushing out on to the landing in the middle of the night in a great state of alarm, saying that there was a man on the roof outside her window. My parents had to re-assure her that it was 'only the owls', but ever afterwards visitors who slept in that room were forewarned.

Between the years 1925 and 1927 I started to make a collection of old birds' nests which I displayed in the summerhouse with the aid of suitable branches. It was my idea of a natural history museum. Once again John Davey took a lively interest, helping me in the identification and adding to it my prize exhibit, a bullfinch's nest. Due to persecution for their depredation of fruit buds, the bullfinches had become very rare and this nest, in a blackthorn hedge, had been a great find. The nest was surprisingly large for the size of the bird, and surprisingly untidy for a finch, being made almost entirely of small twigs.

This was one of the few nests saved when the summerhouse was demolished. Eventually, many years later, it was joined by the exquisite nest of a goldcrest, like a tiny hammock slung beneath a twig of spruce. I found it in Willingham Woods, as I sat in the car and observed the parent birds making many visits to feed the young. Later, when the birds had flown, I was able to return to the woods and retrieve the nest, branch and all. I showed it proudly to a member of our BENA group. He inspected it in silence for some time and then said, 'I promised my wife a fur coat if she could find one of these. She's looked everywhere.'

In some of these activities I had the staunch support of Pip who was a phenomenal tree-climber – much more daring than I. She liked nothing better than to shin up a tree in search of a nest, and the more impossible the tree looked the better she liked it. Things didn't always work out well and there was a time when Pip never seemed to be without bandages or stitches, or a limb in plaster. She had a narrow squeak one day, in the Abbey Woods, when she climbed an ancient beech tree to examine a hole and came face to face with an angry owl. She was very lucky to escape unhurt but, although the episode made her cautious, it didn't make her afraid. Even at that moment of confrontation she couldn't resist looking in the hole so recently vacated before finally climbing down again. 'Three eggs!' she announced trimphantly, while Sykie and I, down below, held our breath.

The Abbey Woods were exceptional in their variety of wildlife of every kind. It was a place quite undisturbed and unfrequented and we loved our visits there, especially in springtime. As we approached across the common we could always be sure of a noisy welcome from the jackdaws who inhabited the old ruined buildings and retaining wall. Alongside this was part of the moat, still filled with water but choked a bit with rushes and fallen branches. Here a pair of waterhens lived and at our approach they would go lurching off across the water, with their funny jerky movements, to find cover in the rushes. We often found the nest because it was not very well concealed, being somewhat raised up on a sort of home-made raft, out of the way of possible floods. They produced a large clutch of pretty brown-blotched eggs and the tiny, fluffy black chicks took to the water almost as soon as they were hatched.

Once through the gate we were into the grassy ride which separated the new wood of larch and spruce from the few remaining beech trees of the old wood; these were gnarled and huge and of such great age that they might have been planted by the monks some four hundred years before. The ride itself had a carpet of flowers in spring, violets and primroses, early purple orchids, bugle and wood anemones – wind flowers we called them. Our knowledge of wild flowers' names was obtained largely from the Flower Fairies series of books. The illustrations we so loved and pored over were sufficiently accurate, botanically, to identify the more common flowers and berries of garden, field and hedgerow. But for the rest there was no book to which we could turn for help. My mother had been keen on wild flowers in her youth and people would say, 'Ask your mother, she'll know.' But when I would rush up to her eagerly with a 'Mummy, Mummy, look what I've found. What is it?' her likely response, almost without looking at what I held in my hand, was, 'Oh! I knew once, but I've forgotten.' It was a great disappointment that no interest was shown and no encouragement given and though Tassie and Sykie would do their best to help, it wasn't the same. 'When I have children,' I thought, 'I'll encourage them and buy them books and show them how to use them.'

Later I studied botany at school and simply loathed it. Flowers were to me a sort of love affair – a series of delightful and intimate discoveries – the places where they grew (sunny or shady, damp or dry) and the company they kept; their shapes and the number of their petals, their colour and their fragrance – especially their fragrance, subtle and precious – making you feel as though by drawing in the scent too greedily you might use it all up. But the last thing I wanted was to learn about flowers in the lab, cutting them in half and examining them under a magnifying glass. That seemed cold, clinical and cruel.

Once, among the ruins of the abbey's domestic buildings, I found a strangle thistle whose shining, holly-green leaves were chased with white veins. Its identity remained an unsolved mystery for many years until I found it again, by the ruins of another abbey. It was the milk thistle, a relic of the monks' medicine garden, also called the holy thistle and used in the treatment of liver and spleen disorders.

Beyond the larch wood the ground begins to drop down to the beck, a stream which once supplied the abbey with clear, running water and was in fact navigable in the thirteenth century when the abbey was being built. I remember several kinds of fish of which the flounder won the prize because it was the biggest and because its marvellous camouflage made it suddenly invisible when it settled on the gravelly bottom – the poor descendants, maybe, of the fish that once stocked the monks' fish ponds, to be eaten on Fridays. It was in the beck, too, that Pip and I later learnt to swim. It is almost impossible to realize that it is now dry and overgrown, as if it had never been, except for the reed-mace and yellow flags that still grow there.

On the bank of the beck, below the larch wood, was a swampy bit known as The Jungle, carpeted with kingcups in spring and thick with willows that had once been grown for basket- and hurdle-making. Here we were sure to hear the plaintive cadence of the willow wren, so sweet and sad a sound.

John Davey was the inspiration behind many of these expeditions. He was up to all sorts of things and his knowledge and curiosity seemed inexhaustible. A favourite trick was to imitate the call of the cuckoo, which he could do with such uncanny accuracy that an answering cuckoo would come looking for him. Another time I discovered a scraping in a hedge bank which seemed to be littered with chewed-up brown paper. John looked at it with interest. 'Hello!' he said, 'We have a badger about. No other creature but a badger will dig out a wasp's nest and eat it.' Throughout his long life he never lost his boyish sense of adventure and enthusiasm and he was always fun to be with. Despite the fact that he was one of my father's generation and had been badly wounded and disfigured in the First World War he, like my grandfather, was one who could meet a child on its own level and it meant a great deal to me.

His Lincolnshire and mine are not what they were. The pastures have been ploughed and the cowslips are gone; hedges where the whitethroat danced have been grubbed up and the owl tree cut down. Winter stubble no longer provides a lifeline for geese or linnets. Cottages that used to teem with life and bulge with children are now either boarded up and derelict or face-lifted beyond recognition, their

Badly hand-knitted owls

double-glazed picture windows making strange companions for mock-Georgian fanlight doors and brass carriage lamps. A few years ago the field in the front of our house at Thornton was sprayed with chemicals from the air. The next day there was an evil-looking scum on the pond at the back of the house and all the goldfish were dead.

Yet nothing is for ever. Even now the tide of public opinion is beginning to swell with the realization that the price of progress has been too high. The gifts of nature may yet return: 'Bring me my bow of burning gold . . .'

Summertime

Summertime

'Ne'er cast a clout till May be out' runs the old adage and in our family it was adhered to as though it were the Eleventh Commandment. It was of no avail to argue that it really meant may, not May, and that it was reasonable to suppose that if may blossom came out early it was because the weather was mild. Granted, May on the east coast tends to be a cold month with the wind still blowing from Siberia, but it seemed ridiculous to be muffled up in winter clothes on a hot day just because it might be cold tomorrow. So we had to endure our Chilprufe vests and liberty bodices, two pairs of knickers and flannel petticoats until 1 June, after which a judicious casting of clouts was allowed.

The arrival of summer prompted all sorts of special activities. The first sign, as predictable as the return of the house martins, was a visit for tea with Miss Robertson at Walk House. Robbie, as we called her, was an elderly lady who kept house for a bachelor farmer and was a friend of my mother. A small, round person with a pleasant smiling face, Robbie wore beautifully old-fashioned clothes – a dress made of stiff black silk with many little tucks and braids – and a black velvet choker round her neck decorated with an amethyst brooch. She loved children and we always looked forward to our visits for all sorts of reasons. For one thing, there was a large flock of Khaki Campbell ducks to be chased into the pond, with a great quacking and splashing. Then there was a very splendid tea.

But first Robbie would say, 'I think those naughty guinea-fowl have been laying away from home. Shall we go and see if we can find them?' and she would lead the way through the little iron gate into the meadow, guiding us craftily to where she knew the nest was in the hedge bottom then allowing us to find it for ourselves. Speckled guinea-fowl eggs for tea were utterly delectable. They were cooked at the table in an ingenious silver egg-boiler, which was like a globe on four legs, hinged at the Equator and opening to reveal four round holes in which the eggs sat over a small reservoir of boiling water. Underneath was a miniature double-sided pan, one side shallow, the other deeper, in which just the right amount of methylated spirit burnt to produce either a lightly done or a hard-boiled egg. Tea was served in a harlequin tea-set and it was one of Robbie's little foibles to see that cup, saucer and plate did *not* match, so that one might get a crimson cup, turquoise saucer and yellow plate. It never failed as a talking point. The meal continued with muffins and cake. And there is a less pleasant, but unforgettable incident involving my first encounter with caraway seed cake. On being offered the plate I chose a large slice, and much regretted my greed. Good manners required me to eat every crumb without indicating by face or behaviour that it was quite the nastiest thing I had ever tasted!

After tea a box of delights appeared from a cupboard. It contained a kaleidoscope for which we collected flower petals from the garden to make the pretty patterns, but we were less enthusiastic about the board games which required counters, as those were in the form of date stones and we didn't know who had sucked them and spat them out!

Picnics were always popular and, although there were not many good picnicking places within walking distance, the grounds of Thornton Abbey were always a favourite. Sykie was a past master at organizing these outings with the maximum spirit of adventure and the minimum fuss. There were special points of interest along the one-mile walk that had to be inspected. They punctuated the way nicely into sections. First came a gnarled old sycamore tree where we used to carry on conversations with the fairies and arrange midnight assignations; next came a patch of hedge where wild gooseberries grew, small, hairy and very sour, then on to the hollow ash tree where a little owl lived and, finally, to a small pond with a bright spring bubbling up through the gravel in one corner where watercress grew. It went well with sardine sandwiches. But the monumental pile of the great Augustine gatehouse lured us on from the moment it came into view.

The public was admitted in the summer months on payment of a small charge but the custodian, who lived in the little lodge behind the gatehouse, would usually let us in free, because we were regulars, and it was not often that we found anyone else there. The few visitors tended to spend their time exploring the gatehouse, which was a grand and extensive building three storeys high, with vast rooms, fireplaces, oriel window and spiral stair turret, where once guests and travellers had been housed, including two kings of England, no less, with their queens and courtiers. But for us it held no surprises. Everything was there to be seen and little imagination was needed to figure out what it had been and how it had been used.

No, we pressed on across the field behind the gatehouse, where few people bothered to go, and there, amid the long grass, brambles and cow parsley, were the sparse ruins of what had been that vast abbey church and its conventual buildings. Over the centuries the place had been systematically quarried for its fine dressed limestone, evidence of which could be seen in buildings in the neighbourhood, including the cellars of our house. Mostly it now consisted of grassy banks with bits of stone sticking through, the bases of a few pillars and an empty stone coffin that we used to lie in to get a funny creepy feeling. The only remains of solid buildings were a transept wall towering crazily out of the greenery, a section of the octagonal chapter house with elaborate blind arcading, and a long narrow room lined all around the walls with stone seats and with a stone vaulted roof. We liked this room because we could always be sure of seeing bats hanging upside-down from the roof. The walls were bright green from the damp and bore the carved or scratched initials of many generations of idle visitors seeking immortality. Piles of rubble and vegetation disguised the rest, so that it required a good imagination to see the abbey – to feel it – as a complex of buildings and to people it with those medieval monks who lived and prayed, sang and laughed, ate and complained of the cold.

It stirred me to reconstruct these unlikely fragments in my mind and I was always looking for 'discoveries'. One such was made in the summer of 1927, just before my tenth birthday. We had been studying, with Sykie, the life of the monasteries up to the Reformation and my curiosity prompted me to climb over the rubble where the cloister had been; there I found just two stone steps of a staircase that had gone. They were quite wide and had been very well used, so that parts of the steps had been worn away by the passage of many feet which had always trodden in exactly the same place. They must have

Discoveries

been part of the stairs from the monks' dormitory over the cloisters, which led down into the church, the monks coming down them so often that they knew the footwork by heart – even in the dark, even in their half-sleep.

In the midst of what had been the cloister garth was an enormous mound of rubble surmounted by a large ash tree. Rabbits had burrowed into the mound and in doing so had exposed pieces of carved and dressed stone which had once formed part of the surrounding buildings. Defying the nettles and brambles that shared the mound with the tree, the rabbits and an occasional lizard, I spent many happy hours engrossed in my 'discoveries', digging and scratching about with a stick to prise out any stones that were small enough to handle. Most of them were just rough infill, the carved stones being too big to be moved by my feeble efforts, but once I found a stone with interesting grooves which, when cleaned off, revealed a scratched drawing of a man's head in a sort of Chaucerian hat with a drape on one side. It was very rough and was, I liked to think, a crude portrait of the works foreman, done by one of the builders and causing a snigger to go round the late fourteenth-century workforce. The thought occurred to me that if that were true, then I was the very first person to set eyes on it since the builders put it in place more than five hundred years before.

Pip did not share my passion for these things. She had probably collected four or five fox-hound puppies being walked at the farms we passed en route and was off on her own hunting expedition, galloping along as though on a horse, with whip and imaginary hunting horn, her 'pack' as keen as mustard. The unfortunate quarry was, most likely, the custodian's small brown dog that looked rather like a half-sized fox. Sykie was fairly relaxed about our activities and managed to see that I didn't fall off a wall while keeping tabs on Pip's hunt to make sure she didn't actually catch Mr Spencer's little dog, without in any way cramping our style and spoiling our fun. The abbey was my private world of romance and history: for as long as I was there I could be a novice or an abbot or an eminent visitor. But there came a day when the owner, the Earl of Yarborough, handed it over to the Office of Works who excavated it and laid it out most beautifully, the loose stones cemented together for safety's sake, the grass mown immaculately and lots of helpful little labels posted explaining everything. And all the magic disappeared. I felt bereft.

Towards the end of July, when the weather seemed settled, the day would come when Mummy announced, 'Tomorrow we are going to Sutton for the day,' and there would be much cheering and prancing about. Sutton-on-Sea was a favourite seaside place about an hour's drive from home. And for the day, the *whole day*! Almost at once we were diving into cupboards where we remembered stowing away the buckets and spades, the shrimping net and the kite – not forgetting the string – after last year's outing. The excitement nearly robbed us of our sleep and by half past eight the next morning we were almost ready, marching about the house chanting, 'We're going to Sutton!

We're going to Sutton!' By nine o'clock Mummy was just emerging for breakfast.

'Mummy, can we go *now?*'

'Oh, wait a minute, wait a minute. There's a lot to do first. I've got to make the sandwiches.'

Cook didn't approve of Mummy going and messing about in the kitchen and why Mummy always insisted on making the sandwiches herself is a mystery. She wasn't the most practical person and cooking was not her strongest point. I remember once finding a recipe for scones, in my mother's handwriting, which read, 'Take half a pint of milk, beat it to a batter and roll it out on a floured board.' Cook and the kitchen-maid were kept scurrying about fetching this and that while Mummy changed her mind half a dozen times and dirtied every knife, fork, spoon, plate and bowl in the kitchen. There were boiled egg sandwiches with mayonnaise, ham sandwiches with chutney, fish paste sandwiches with mustard and cress, malt bread and fruit cake, oranges and bananas, Thermoses of tea and bottles of lemon barley water and ginger beer in brown stoneware bottles. And it all took *ages*.

The morning dragged by interminably and we were fit to burst with frustration by the time the hamper was packed up and loaded into the car and Mummy had gone back a couple of times for things she'd forgotten. But finally we were off, Tassie driving and I sharing the front seat with Mummy because I was almost sure to be car-sick (a tiresome tendency which was to punctuate most of our family outings). My mother never learnt to drive, saying, 'There are enough fools on the road without me.' Sykie, Honor, Pip and the dog were squashed into the back seat with as much clobber as though we were going away for a fortnight. A change of clothes in case we got wet, lots of woollies in case we got cold, bathing things, deck chairs, the hamper, shrimping net with an extremely awkward handle that got in everybody's way, etc., etc.

After Louth the road soon dropped down from the Wolds to the vast coastal marshes where hedges gave way to drainage ditches and the few stunted tree were ironed off at sharp angles by the east wind. One could not see the sea but a great cheer went up as the line of sand-dunes was spotted – and we knew from experience the exact spot where we should see them for the first time – green and gold in the sunshine. Then at last, at last we were there, racing to the top of the bank for the first glimpse of the sea. The relief, as we stood there and surveyed the scene in an all-embracing glance, was almost as great as if we had feared that it might have gone since last year. But it was all there, just as we remembered it – the little white beach huts dotted along the dunes, the golden-white sands, the old wooden breakwaters with their seaweed and pools, and somewhere out there the sea itself, either pounding the beach with a roar or, if the tide was at its lowest, appearing like a glittering line of tinsel in the far distance. *And the smell*! We filled our lungs with great, life-enhancing draughts of it.

'Mummy, can we bathe now?'

'No, later. It's time for lunch. Aren't you hungry?'

So out came the rugs and the hamper and the sandwiches. It was quite a performance but at last it was over and our whole day at the seaside was about to begin.

'Mummy, can we bathe now?'

'No, not for an hour. You've only just had your lunch and it's very bad for you to go in the water with a full stomach.'

Never mind, there were plenty of other things to do. If the tide was coming in we'd make a sand castle, with a moat and a channel to meet the water. There were spades and spades. Small children only had wooden spades, which were relatively ineffectual but safe. Bigger children had metal spades which were beautifully efficient but could chop your toes off – I remember my pride and pleasure at being allowed my first metal spade at the age of eight or so. If the tide was going out then the breakwaters were the place to be, with net and bucket, finding shrimps and small crabs left behind in the pools. And eventually we got our bathe, though it only consisted of jumping the waves and messing about in the shallows. We couldn't swim.

All too soon it was time to go home, with our collection of shells and seaweed, the bucket of shrimps that usually managed to get tipped over, and with blisters on our heels from wearing new sand-shoes – last year's being too small. And although we really did enjoy it, I used to make a solemn vow to myself, 'When I have children we shall have a *whole day* at the beach. And there won't, *ever*, be any sandwiches.'

With grandparents living on the edge of the Lake District we spent some happy holidays there in the days when Windermere was relatively peaceful and when the road to Tarn Hows was a gated farm track.

The journey took all day, because there were always stops for me to be sick, for the picnic lunch, and for the routine inspection of the Ebb-and-Flow Well at Giggleswick, in the hope of seeing it flow (we never did). The landscape changed slowly and subtly – the contours, the shapes, the colours and the buildings. Green hedges gave way to grey walls, red brick turned to stone and the land changed from brown and green to blue and purple. First we travelled through country criss-crossed by a network of canals and waterways where it was a common but intriguing sight to see a coal barge making its way with only the handsome red-brown canvas sail visible above the bank, so that it looked as though it were sailing through a field. Later we passed through Selby with its imposing abbey church so similar in ground plan and in size to our own Thornton Abbey. Could Thornton ever have looked so magnificent? A few miles beyond Selby we passed through Monk Fryston, so called because all the stone to build Selby Abbey was quarried there. My mind peopled the place with busy quarry-workers and stone masons and the men with their trundling ox-carts who hauled the stone the eight miles back to Selby. Further on again was a small coal-mining town where retired miners would congregate on the street corner, squatting on their heels because, having been in that position all their working lives, it was more comfortable than standing upright.

As we approached Ilkley the first moors appeared, bright with heather in full bloom, prompting us to burst into those lines from 'All things bright and beautiful' which go, 'The purple headed mountains, The river running by . . .'. Nothing spelled out the differences of the landscape more clearly than the appearance of rocky outcrops sticking up through the grass. Here was God-made country that man, 'proud man, drest in a little brief authority', had learnt to live with but had not been able to rub out and draw again.

Even the most cherished landscapes were not quite enough to occupy us for the whole journey and there were various games we used to play to pass the time. One was to count horses, of which there were always plenty both in the fields and on the roads. Piebalds or skewbalds counted double and the first to reach a hundred was the winner, but anyone who saw a donkey had to go back to the beginning and start again. A better game was called 'Post Offices' with a points system involving some intricate arithmetic – one for a postman on foot, two for a postman on a bicycle, three for a pillar-box on a wall, four for a free-standing pillar-box and five for a post office. In later years it was possible to add telephone kiosks and mail-vans. Only the person who saw the item first was allowed to count it and cheating was very definitely not on – even about the donkey.

Grannie and Grandpa Mawson lived at Caton then, not far from Lancaster where Grandpa had his office. He was a great plantsman and of all the honours bestowed upon him his fellowship of the Linnean Society was the one he most prized. One of his loves were the big tuberous begonias and at Caton there was a large, round flowerbed in the lawn filled with these exotic flowers. First thing every morning I went to inspect the bed to see if any of the big flower-heads had snapped off. The casualties would be cradled in my hands and I could hardly bear to part with them, they were so beautiful. Eventually a flat glass bowl would be found for them and a nice green leaf or two to keep them company.

Much of the holiday was spent in and around their lovely big garden, with trees to climb, fairy glades to explore with Grandpa and the Crook of Lune only 200 yards from the front gate. The Crook of Lune was a magical place if ever there was one. Here the River Lune sweeps round in a huge bend leaving a sandy beach on the near side (reached by a kissing gate and a little path across a meadow) and, against the steeply wooded bank on the far side, deep, dark water from which fish would leap and plunge back with a plop, making bright rings that slowly widened.

Behind the house the moors of the Pennines rose up to the sharp, high profile of Clougha (pronounced Cloffer) and the winding moorland road led past the millstone-grit quarries at Quernmore (perversely pronounced Quormer), so called because from those very quarries the Romans cut and worked the stone into hand querns for grinding corn. It was still possible, in the 1920s, to find stones which had broken during working and been abandoned. I have seen many such querns in museums since and always the thought has entered my mind, 'I wonder if they came from Quernmore?' Then the road took us up the valley, climbing higher and higher, to the Trough of Bowland with its brilliant mountain stream tumbling about among the boulders, fringed with pine trees and mossy banks, where I tickled my first trout.

But, of course, there were always days spent in Lakeland itself. Mummy came to life in her native countryside and although she professed to find the mountains claustrophobic and preferred the wide open spaces of Lincolnshire, nevertheless she was happy to show off her intimate knowledge of the place. We would visit her favourite haunts and she would show us how to find fresh-water crayfish which hid under the stones in shallow streams. And it was fun to drink the water, provided we first walked a hundred yards upstream (and back) to make sure there was no dead animal to pollute it. Occasionally, Mummy would have her doubts when a stream appeared even more crystal clear than usual, and we would not be allowed to drink from it in case it contained lead.

One particularly memorable and bizarre occasion sticks in my mind. We were the guests of Uncle Edward who planned to take us for a picnic up the Langdale Pikes as far as Easdale Tarn. Uncle Edward, my mother's eldest brother, was a great favourite. He was a very funny man, rotund, with a face like Humpty-Dumpty and eyebrows that made him look permanently surprised. He was full of tricks and good humour and interesting anecdotes. An architect and town planner by profession, he had received part of his education at L'Ecôle des Beaux Arts in Paris and was a dedicated francophile, sporting a jaunty bow-tie which was then considered arty and un-English. My father regarded the exposure of shirt buttons as embarrassing, if not indelicate, and quite as bad as a woman showing her petticoat. But the bow-tie gave Uncle Edward a certain Left-Bank style which he demonstrated admirably on this occasion.

The two cars were left at the farm at the foot of the path and, lugging a number of baskets along with us, we set off on our climb. At first the going was easy, but soon the path steepened as we negotiated Sour Milk Gill, the white water scrambling rather than plunging down its wide rock face and the pebbles loose and slippery. We paused to look back at the valley far below and at our two cars like tiny toys, then we resumed our climb which soon became less steep and breathtakingly beautiful. Finally we arrived at the tarn, tired and relieved to be able to stop.

Here Uncle Edward discovered a conveniently flat rock which would

A day at the seaside

serve as a table and proceeded to prepare the meal. Sandwiches? Not on your life! First out of the basket was a red-and-white checked table-cloth which was spread over the rock. Next came a neat little stove on which he grilled chicken joints in a mustard sauce, and served them with a fresh green salad tossed in French dressing made on the spot with an impressive display of abracadabra. This was accompanied by two bottles of what I suspect was Chablis, which had been parked in the stream to cool while the preparations were going on. Altogether it was a masterly display of organization and finesse and had a distinctly Impressionist atmosphere about it. Judging by the grown-ups, who giggled all afternoon, it was a great success. But Uncle

Edward still had energy to spare and a trick to show us children. He was a keen fisherman (mainly to escape from his talkative wife) and taking some bread and one of the willow baskets that had held the picnic, he stepped out on to a stone which rose like a little island out of the tarn. Crumbling the bread in his hand he cast it upon the waters. Immediately a large shoal of little fish appeared as if from nowhere, shattering the still surface into a seething frenzy as they fought for the bread. Deftly Uncle Edward scooped the basket through the water and, hey presto, he had thirty or forty little silver fish all leaping about in it. Of course, when we had had a good look at them he put them back and they disappeared just as suddenly as they had come.

Other details of that fabulous day are blurred. Who went on the trip? I don't remember. Was the journey down to the cars difficult for our young legs? Pip would only have been six. All gone. But what lingers very clearly in the memory is a day of days when nothing was like anything we had ever done before; when grown-ups had actually laughed all day long and Uncle Edward was a hero from a fairy tale that came true.

As summer came to an end and days began to shorten there were 'last rites' to be performed before the season could be allowed to die. Blackberrying was Mummy's passion and she was very good at it. Blackberry and apple pie, with Stilton cheese, was Daddy's passion, so when September arrived there was bound to be at least one final picnic. Scawby was reckoned the best place, not only because the blackberries were plentiful and the beautiful heathland where they grew accessible, but also because it was not far enough for me to be sick – always a consideration. The quiet lane that ran through the area had broad grass verges clipped to a fine lawn by rabbits and studded with little carpets of wild thyme. Beyond lay the sandy heathland with silver birch and larch, heather and brambles, and much more waiting to be discovered. It was a place full of fascination and surprises.

As soon as picnic tea was over Mummy began the real business of the outing, using the now empty sandwich boxes as containers for the blackberries. We were all supposed to help, but after a short while we children found other things that took our attention. We might see a lizard or a slow-worm – there was no knowing what might be revealed to the observant. Mummy by this time was well into her stride and her answers to calls of 'Mummy, where are you?' came from further and further away. The successful filling of the sandwich boxes was supposed to prescribe the limits of the expedition, but just at that moment she usually found a simply marvellous new place. So pockets and handbags were turned out in search of envelopes which she made into little boxes by folding the bottom corners. As light began to fade and the rugs and picnic basket had been loaded into the car, Daddy began to grow anxious and went off in search of her. His 'Time to call it a day' was countered with 'Oh, but look! I can't leave these; they're the best I've seen all day. Have you a box of matches?' And she would finish her blackberrying by the light of one match after another till the box was empty.

And so summer drifted imperceptibly into autumn, leaving behind it illusions of long days of endless sunshine and fun, bird-song, flowers and butterflies. After crowding the telegraph wires for days, the house martins suddenly departed, leaving behind them the empty mud nests above the nursery window and a strange quietness.

Winter clothes appeared from their hiding places smelling strongly of moth-balls and it was time to look for conkers. The clocks went back (we never had any difficulty in remembering whether they went 'back' or 'on' because in Lincolnshire autumn is known by the unlovely epithet Back End – the clocks went back at Back End) and picnics gave way to toast and dripping by the nursery fire.

Christmas

Christmas

Is Christmas more commercialized than it was? Yes, of course it is in the sense that there is more pressure on us all to spend, spend, spend. Advertisements seriously cajole us to buy diamonds, conservatories, swimming pools and cars for presents and, for the children, catalogues tell them that the bike of their dreams is *only* £199.95. 'Look, Dad, it's *only* £199.95.' Expectations are high. Mustn't disappoint the children.

On the other hand the reminders of what is being celebrated are everywhere more in evidence than they used to be. There is no escaping Christmas carols in shops and on television and radio, Christmas cribs in every church, nativity plays in every primary school and Christmas cards depicting people going to church in the snow, choirboys in frilly surplices, the Three Kings, shepherds watching their flocks, angels trumpeting the good news and the Good News itself, manger, animals, star, the lot. These are new. And though they may have no religious depth to them at least they are there for those who wish to celebrate Christmas as a religious festival. The saddest fate that can befall Christmas is not that it becomes a pagan feast but that it becomes a chore. Oh, the cost of it all and the shopping, the work, and the grumbling – '*my poor feet*!' But what makes Christmas special is the rejoicing of the heart and all the rest stems from that. If the heart is too tired to rejoice then one has got it wrong.

The story of the Nativity as told by St Luke was well beloved by us and we knew most of it by heart. But I have no recollection of anything Christmassy happening in our church. Carol services had not been invented, Midnight Mass was strictly for Roman Catholics; a crib with figures would have been idolatrous. Christmas trees and evergreens were at best secular, at worst heathen. (What about harvest festival?) White chrysanthemums on the altar were as far as decorations went. There was no children's service, although we were bidden, on the Sundays in Advent, to think of poor and sick children and to collect toys and books for hospitals and orphanages. I remember shutting my eyes tight during prayers and seeing awful visions of the boys from the local orphanage float before me – the nearest I got to prayer, I suppose. It was a nightmare place, a large, barren Victorian building with curtainless windows like the empty eye-sockets of a skull. The boys were unbelievably gaunt and pale and wretched as they walked two by two in the charge of an equally cadaverous master, with rimless spectacles, his cane always at the ready. What sort of Christmas did they have?

No, so far as the church was concerned, rejoicing was not the name of the game, or, if it were, then they had a funny way of showing it. The only service on Christmas Day was Holy Communion at 8 a.m., which a few zealous and serious-minded people attended, sombrely dressed, eyes down, hands clasped. As a child the thought of Communion made me feel uncomfortable. It was never talked about, but I knew that to attend it you had to be a member of a secret society and undergo strange initiation rites. It involved cannibalism. This much was clear from the service which I had read surreptitiously during sermons. To me it seemed offensive and revolting. No wonder they found the burden of their sins intolerable. If it was so wicked, why did they do it? And what happened to Gentle Jesus meek and mild who was a friend of little children? Questions, questions, but there was never anyone to answer.

Well, let's leave the church and get on with Christmas. For us children Christmas was the pinnacle of the long, dark winter and had, I seem to remember, a slightly Nordic paganism about it. The build-up was slow and leisurely, spread over many weeks, at first not directly or obviously related to Christmas itself. Autumn could not be hurried; it would take its time and go through its phases. This was the season to think of logs for the fire, when the thin white mists hung about the wood and obscured Frogmore Farm and the view beyond from our nursery window. Then the still air would be invaded by the ring of the woodman's axe (a beautiful sound) while the crackling bonfire of brushwood sent a spiralling column of blue smoke up through the mist and added the fragrance of burning wood to the special autumn smell of damp leaves.

Daddy used to buy a truck-load of logs which arrived in a big lorry and were stacked away in the woodshed. But these were ordinary logs for ordinary fireplaces and for the Christmas season the dining-room table, extended to its full length, was moved into the hall where there was an open hearth requiring logs two or three feet long. As these could not be bought in the usual way one of our own trees was felled and it would be all hands to the task for several weekends, working with axe and wedges for splitting, cross-cut saw for a strenuous two-man job and the all-important sawing-horse across which the wood was laid for cutting. There was enough work to keep everybody warm on the coldest Saturday and, although there was not much we children could do but get in the way, the feeling of team-work and togetherness and the practical outcome of the effort was highly satisfactory. In later years I liked nothing better than to be on one end of the cross-cut saw, swinging to a rhythm that was like poetry.

Then came a day in late November when we were summoned to the kitchen to stir the Christmas pudding and to make a wish. There was never any stirring about it because the mixture was so stiff that all one could do was prod it with the wooden spoon and turn over a bit of it hopefully, though I always felt that my wish was adversely affected by not being properly stirred. Our puddings were mixed in a huge earthenware crock, known as a pancheon, in which the bread was usually made. The pudding to be eaten on Christmas Day had little silver charms in it. Bachelor's button, spinster's thimble, wish-bone, cat, threepenny bit and wedding ring, these were wrapped in tiny parcels of greaseproof paper and tied with cotton (so that we didn't swallow them accidentally) and inserted evenly with a knife after the first boiling.

By the beginning of December the pace was hotting up. Pip and I were busy with private lists that no one must see and looking forward to our one and only shopping spree to Grimsby. As we made all our gifts, cards and calendars ourselves there was little actual shopping to be done, but Christmas would not have been Christmas without the added excitement of the trip. There were no street decorations, but shops put on a brave display. Poulterers' were hung on the outside with every kind of feathered fowl, barrow-boys sold holly and mistletoe from carts in the streets, green-grocers overflowed with nuts, figs, dates and pineapples. Above all we loved to accompany Mummy to the leading grocer where she placed her Christmas order. It was a lovely shop which first drew attention to itself by roasting coffee-beans in a machine in the window. The wheels went round and sparks flew out and a great deal of smoke drifted out into the streets, carrying its delectable smell to all who passed by. Why does coffee smell so much nicer than it tastes?

Inside the shop there were more delights. Displays of ginger in pretty blue-and-white jars, crystallized fruits all gooey in their smart wooden boxes with lace-like paper edges and, oh, the boxes of crackers! Everything from miniatures to the most exotic creations that were far too beautiful to pull.

Then there was the overhead system that carried the money to the cashier in little containers on wires. When the lever was pulled the container went off on its journey with a ping. At busy times such as Christmas they were pinging about all over the shop. They travelled so fast that Pip and I had difficulty in keeping up with them and we were not at all popular when we crashed into silly people who got in our way.

Ah, but another treat was still in store. At the back of the shop, through the glass swing-doors, was a café in which a real live trio played real live music, up on a little dais, flanked by palm trees in pots. They played 'In a Monastery Garden', Handel's Largo and Gilbert and Sullivan and sometimes hits from the latest musicals. To us, sitting there with our feet on red carpet, eating outsized cream cakes of unimaginable confection while gazing raptly at the contortions of the instrumentalists, it seemed another world – a sheik of Araby couldn't have wished for more.

We returned home in high spirits and must start there and then. What should we make for Daddy? What about a little chest-of-drawers made of four match-boxes covered with wallpaper and containing paper-clips, drawing-pins and suchlike for his office desk? Mummy? Mummy was singularly hard to impress and the badly sewn handkerchief with rather grubby lace round the edge would go into a drawer never to be seen again. Tassie, on the other hand, would treasure her equally badly made pin-cushion as though it were the crown jewels, and it would be in daily use on her dressing-table for years to come.

Christmas cards were very different then. For one thing they were rarely religious. I believe religious cards were popularized at a later date by the Medici Society's reproductions of old masters' nativity paintings. But in the 1920s the cards were more likely to show robins and holly, children on toboggans, Dickensian family feasts and mail coaches struggling through snow-drifts. They were about fun and cheer and had nothing to do with either good taste or virgin births. Even the way cards were made was different. They consisted of two pages, the outer page of stiffish card with the picture on the front and the inner page of paper with the written message, both pages held together by a ribbon tied in a bow on the edge. Our home-made cards followed this formula as faithfully as possible, sometimes with our own paintings, but what we liked best was to use 'scraps' which could be bought in sheets and showed pretty little girls in button boots and fur muffs, baskets of roses, birds' nests with eggs – not in the least Christmassy but bright and eye-catching.

I don't ever remember carol singers coming round to the house, but we did sing carols round the piano and 'Good King Wenceslas' was the clear favourite. It had a good story-line, a commendable moral and evocative words. I liked the picture conjured up by 'In his master's steps he trod, where the snow lay dinted.' Who has not done that?

In other times, before the First World War, there had been a mummers' play performed in Wootton and we loved to hear Margie Swallow recite it for our benefit at Christmas time. She knew all the parts and could imitate beautifully the country voices who spoke them, as she remembered them from her childhood. There was the carpenter, together with the milkman and the butcher's man and half a dozen others, playing the parts they and their forebears had jealously guarded for – how long? Centuries? Parts with names like Sir Christmas, the Turkish Knight and Saint George who, of course, slew the Turkish Knight in a great sword fight at the end. Though ours had to be a second-hand account, Margie's story-telling ability was such that I can see all those people in my mind even now and it has always been a regret that I did not learn the words from her while I had the chance.

Excitement increased with the arrival of an evening when we wrote our lists for Father Christmas. It was understood that these were stocking presents we were asking for and it was not polite to be greedy and grasping. That did not discourage Pip from writing 'Dear Father Christmas, Please may I have a real pack of hounds and a pony and a hunting horn and a . . .' She did manage to get a set of lead hunting figures, including a fox, to go with our treasured farm set, and a real hunting horn which she learnt to sound quite proficiently. I preferred paints, crayons, sewing things and books. Then we would see our bits of paper go fluttering up the drawing-room chimney. We knew Father Christmas was up there waiting for them because we could hear all sorts of strange noises in the chimney and we would shout messages up to him, telling him to be careful.

A few days before Christmas Watson, the gardener, appeared – pom, pa-pom, pa-pom' – up the path nearly bent double under an enormous bundle of evergreens. There were branches of holly, laurel and bay, sprigs of yew and box, and ivy. Mummy produced a large ball of string and we all set to work to make long swags to reach from the four corners of the main rooms to the lamp chain in the middle. The twelve-foot Christmas tree in the corner of the hall was decorated by our parents after we had gone to bed and was a glittering surprise for us in the morning.

And at last came Christmas Eve itself, which dragged slowly by and had to be assisted by chestnuts roasted on the bars of the drawing-room fire and stories and games. Then, finally, it was time to put Father Christmas's glass of sherry and mince-pie on the nursery hearth, fix our stockings to the bed-posts and try to settle down. But strange things were stirring and there was magic in the air. We lay there, our ears straining to catch the merest sound of hooves on the slates, the rustle of a sackful of parcels in the profound silence, or even the distant sound of angels' voices singing 'Glory to God in the highest'. It was a night when *anything* could happen. We tried to keep awake, half determined to see Father Christmas, half terrified that he would know we were only pretending to be asleep and so not come at all. One Christmas I awoke to find Father Christmas in the room, moving stealthily about from the end of my bed to Pip's, and to hear the soft but unmistakable sound of rustling paper. By half-opening one eye I could just make out the bulky outline of a large man muffled up in a cloak. My heart was thumping against my ribs so uncomfortably that I felt sure he *must* be able to hear it. After he had gone I crept out from under my warm bedclothes and groped about in the dark for the stocking, just to make *sure*. Yes, there it was: apple, something hard, soft, orange, soft, cracker, square box. Now I could sleep till morning.

'HE'S BEEN!' The cry shattered the dawn and Christmas had begun. The mood of Christmas Day was noticeably different from what had gone before. After the long wait, with all its tension, here at last was the pure pleasure of realization. We carried our stockings in triumph to our parents' big double bed and sneaked in under the eiderdown. Of all the joys of Christmas nothing quite matched up to the stocking. What was it about the stocking? Was it the magic element of Father Christmas himself? Was it the uncertainty – that he *might* not come? But he *had* come – 'O frabjous day! Callooh! Callay!'

Woolly cap and gloves, just what I wanted and the right colour too; how clever of him! And a little metal chicken coop with a door that really opened and there inside was a mother hen with lots of little yellow chicks – a great addition to our farm set. Oh, and pencils and crayons and drawing book, *and* pencil sharpener *and* rubber. Goodness, he's thought of everything! Cleverly, Father Christmas usually managed to include some simple game or construction toy that kept us busy and happy until breakfast time. And I cannot remember Pip ever being shattered with disappointment at not finding a pack of hounds in her stocking, or if she had ever quite worked out in her mind how she thought they might get in there.

In the hall the big logs were already blazing on the great stone hearth and breakfast was all the more special because of the piles of parcels staring at us from under the tree. But we must wait and contain our curiosity and excitement a little longer until breakfast was finished and cleared away and we had completed our few nursery chores. Then the moment of the grand opening had arrived.

Before all the razzmatazz of modern packaging had been invented – pretty wrapping paper, made-up bows and fancy labels – we were perfectly content with brown paper and string. Occasionally our imagination would have a little flutter with crêpe paper, and very special items might even come wrapped in white tissue paper tied with real ribbon. For a week or more the house had been full of secrets and the rustle of paper. There were furtive goings-on behind the sofa and cries of 'Don't look!' Certain places became no-go areas – Mummy's dressing-room, for instance. But now the waiting was over and the great moment had come. Soon we were knee-deep in brown paper and string, greeting each new discovery with cries of delight, while Mummy made valiant efforts, not always successful, to list things before gift and label became irrevocably separated, because thank-you letters were a *must*. Even now recollections come flooding back of some of the real winners. One year it was wooden cots for our ever-growing nursery 'family', the product of Daddy's workshop and many secret hours of craftsmanship, with bedclothes that included lace-edged pillow-cases and silk eiderdowns made by Mummy. On another occasion it was a beautiful model farmhouse and range of farm-buildings, with outside steps up to the granary, just like those at Frogmore, also Daddy's work, which were supplemented by some very cunning farm hedges and trees made by Mummy from loofah dyed green and cut into shapes.

On the whole, we much preferred home-made presents to bought ones because they were more personal and unique. One exception to this was a perfect little fan made of pink feathers which came from an uncle who had a rare gift for choosing lovely feminine presents for little girls. It was one of the prettiest things I ever possessed and I adored it.

Books were very popular, particularly animal stories, or tales that made your flesh creep, like *Treasure Island*, *Knock Three Times* and *The Midnight Folk*. Annuals were also a great fund of pleasure, especially *Tiger Tim* and a series called the *Joy Street* annuals. We started at *Number One Joy Street* and moved on up the street until we were in double figures. They were very superior annuals, nicely bound in sprig-printed linen, a different colour each year, and the stories, poems, snippets of nature study and things to make and do were definitely a large cut above the rest.

We carried off our treasures to the nursery where a whole host of new possibilities opened up. There was plenty to keep us out of the way until the gong sounded for dinner. The decoration of the dining-table, and in particular the centre-piece, was Mummy's most outstanding contribution to the Christmas scene. It might be a pyramid of fruit and gilded pine-cones fit to grace a Roman bacchanalia, or a dazzling array of lighted candles and glass baubles. Once it was an enchanting scene from 'Cinderella', glass coach glittering with silver paper and four tiny white ponies. I remember particularly a skating scene with whitened trees reflected in the 'ice' (an oval mirror) and little skating figures made of pipe-cleaners and dressed in scarlet, some single with hands clasped behind their backs, some in pairs gliding along sedately, still others engaged in figure-skating. Mummy knew what she was doing, for she was a good skater herself and her deft fingers fashioned the tiny people with great vigour and style. In addition to the centre-piece there were crackers and lots of little bon-bon dishes containing nuts and raisins, Turkish Delight, chocolates, stuffed dates, salted almonds and crystallized ginger. What is more, we were allowed to help ourselves to them whenever we wanted – an absolutely unheard-of indulgence!

Nowadays, when children eat sweets and drink orange squash every day of the year, and a turkey comes out of the deep-freeze for any family occasion, it is hard to realize the simply astonishing experience these once-a-year treats afforded. To my mind a bronze-feathered, farm-reared Norfolk turkey is the noblest bird ever to come to the table. With its traditional accompaniments of stuffing (*never* containing sage), sausage-meat (*always* containing sage) and bread sauce (cranberry sauce is a modern American importation), it presents a plateful of subtle blends of taste and texture, and gains much in stature through being associated only with Christmas Day.

The arrival of the pudding was something of a ritual. George prepared it in his pantry, which led directly into the hall, with a nice sprig of berried holly sticking in the top and a generous pouring of brandy to keep it flaming for at least a minute. With the blue flames licking round the pud and holly crackling merrily as it burned, it was carried to the table shoulder high and with great solemnity, while cheering and clapping broke out all round. Who would get the wedding ring and who would get the thimble? Finally, it was time for crackers and paper hats, riddles and mottoes with which the most memorable meal imaginable was over for another year. We children retired to the nursery to look at our new books while the grown-ups had coffee in the drawing-room and the staff settled down in the servants' hall at three o'clock in the afternoon to enjoy their Christmas dinner – flaming pud, crackers and all. The rest of the day passed quietly and happily – a walk in the afternoon, perhaps, to see what the Bratby children had got. There too, were knitted caps made by Mum

The arrival of the pudding

and wooden toys made by Dad, with maybe a book for Ruby who would treasure it, and a whip and top for Teddy who would show us how to use it and might even let us have a go.

I have always believed in Father Christmas and I always shall. Regardless of who drinks the sherry and eats the mince-pie on the hearth, the Spirit of Mid-winter is, I'm sure, as old as mankind and as real as we want to make it. It represents the first stirrings of man's understanding of the mysteries of the universe. As the year turns the corner it is natural to rejoice in the signs of renewal and hope, whether they be the promise of lengthening days and swelling buds, or of a newborn baby, and whether we mark the occasion with feasting or gifts of gold, frankincense and myrrh. The wise fathers of the early Christian Church knew what they were doing when they superimposed the birthday of Christ on a feast already so ancient and hallowed that there was no way it could be obliterated.

The Twelve Days

The Twelve Days

There was only one place to be on Boxing Day and that was at the meet of the Brocklesby Hunt at Newsham Lodge. It was a perfect setting for a big social gathering, the mock Gothic gateway providing a romantic backdrop and the endless acres of Brocklesby Park, studded with majestic oak trees and surrounded by woods, giving enough room for everybody, their animals and their vehicles. Everyone was there: the earl (in 'pink'), his countess and their daughters on their immaculate, well-bred hunters, the gentry and the farmers, the farmer's boy on the milk-float cob and little girls on fat, shaggy ponies. If you had four legs you rode to hounds on Boxing Day. Hunting did not have the snobbery attached to it then which it has since acquired. It was a widely approved country sport and the ownership of a horse, or pony for the children, was widespread. Where, perhaps, money told most was whether you rode your horse to the meet yourself or whether the groom rode it, leading a spare horse on a rein, while you arrived by car in the nick of time.

Several ladies, including the countess, rode side-saddle looking the picture of elegance in their long skirts, wasp-waisted jackets and tricorn hats so tightly tied on with veiling that the tips of their noses were white from the pressure. The elegance usually only lasted while they were stationary, for at a canter most of them looked like sacks of potatoes and made us laugh – for which our parents rebuked us with loud shush-es.

The Brocklesby fox-hounds were famous and distinctive. Reputed to be the oldest pack in the country, the hounds were easily distinguished by the evenness of their markings – black saddle and strong three-coloured pattern of the head – and by the fact that newborn puppies had a little bit snipped off the tips of their ears to make them square instead of pointed. It was *our* hunt and we were inordinately proud of it. Pip and I liked nothing better than to be in the midst of the hounds, who were affectionate creatures and used to this sort of adulation, and to get to know them individually by name – Handy and Hasty, Leda and Lady.

It was quite alright to follow the hunt on foot so long as you knew the lingo. Hounds waved their sterns – never dogs wagged their tails, while foxes had neither sterns nor tails but brushes. And, of course, the huntsmen did not *really* wear red coats, though how anyone could imagine that the colour was really 'pink' takes some figuring out. We did a lot of following on foot because we never had a pony of our own, though Pip soon proved herself to be such a good horsewoman that she had little difficulty in borrowing a mount from time to time. As for me, I steered well clear of the beasts, who seemed to be unpredictable if not downright malicious. They were not too bad in the middle, if you could manage to stay there, but neither end was to be trusted. Pip was fearless and adored hunting: I pretended to like it but secretly sided with the fox.

Although the *hoi polloi* regarded the Boxing Day Meet as a national sporting occasion, along with Derby Day and the Cup Final, the hunt people had no doubts that it was nothing of the sort. The name of the game was to see and be seen. The atmosphere was friendly: everybody spoke to everybody else and wished them the compliments of the season. It was good publicity for the hunt and a good day out for the rest, but sport it was not. The vast crowds of enthusiasts on foot prided themselves on being able to keep up, while the hunt drew the nearest wood to enable them to do just that. And when a fox broke cover people ran about wildly waving their arms and halloo-ing to turn the wretched animal back towards the pursuing hounds. 'Sheer bloody murder!' as the huntsman said in disgust. But the crowd would not be satisfied until they had been in at the kill, after which they started to drift away home and the hunt could at last strike off for the open country in the hope of a good run.

For my father it was rather a sad reminder of the sport he could no longer enjoy, though there were always some cronies he had known in his hunting days before the war with whom he could pass the time of day. And he would be prompted to tell us tales he remembered from

Boxing Day meet

those days. He had once had a horse that suffered so badly from rheumatism that he had to have a sling and hoist rigged up in the stable to take the horse's weight off its legs at night. The vet said the horse *must* be exercised every day, no matter how little or how slowly, or it would seize up altogether. One day my father had coaxed the horse, painfully, step by step, as far as Bradley Crossroads when the hounds came by in full cry. The horse pricked up its ears and took off, keeping up with the hunt till they killed ninety minutes later. When the excitement was over the horse collapsed and had to be carted home.

The horse lived to hunt another day, but those animals that reached the end of the line went to the Brocklesby Hunt Kennels as food for the hounds. One such old mare was commemorated in a local folk-song which used to be sung in Wootton by an old groom called Herbert. I just remember Herbert, groom to Margie Swallow's father in his hunting days, as a very old wizened little man, but he had been quite a lad in his day, full of 'horse magic', broom-dances and folk-songs. The tune was monotonous but enlivened by its dotted rhythm:

Peter Walker had an old mare,
Her legs were long and her ribs were bare.
He took the old mare to Lincoln Fair
A-thinkin he could sell her there,
But he brought her back. Oh yes he did,
Because he'd never a farthing bid.

He took the old mare to Dunkirk Wood
A-thinkin there she would do some good
But she run with 'er 'ead all in a tree.
'Baa gom,' said Peter, 'th' old mare'll dee.'
He gave her some treakil all in a spuin
And she licked her lips all the afternuin.

He took her some corn all in a sieve
'Baa gom,' said Peter, 'th' old mare'll live.'

At this point Herbert's memory failed him and he would say:

'Owsomever the old mare died.

Then he was off again:

'E dug an 'ole six foot deep
And his wife came out and began to weep
Kind friends let this a warning be . . .

and here Herbert's voice trailed away and the last three barely remembered lines were spoken:

Gi yer 'osses plenty t'eat
Or you can bet yer clogs
They'll atta goo te Brocklesby dogs.

No Christmas season could be allowed to pass without a visit to the pantomime. The pantomimes of my youth are remembered with the very greatest affection. There, before our very eyes, our favourite fairy stories would come to life with all the magic and glamour and glitter the heart could desire. We used to go to Hull because that was considered the best show within reach. It also provided an exciting day out, requiring a half-hour journey across the Humber in a paddle steamer. This was a rather grand ship, having an upper deck, a lower deck and a deck for cars, a first-class cabin, a third-class cabin and serving refreshments. But our favourite place was down below, where we could see the great pistons working and hear the swish-swish-swish of the paddles as they thrashed through the chocolate-brown water. Sometimes, when the tide was low, the steamer was obliged to go a long way round to avoid the sandbanks. When the paddles turned slower and slower it was time to race up on deck to watch the crewman swinging the lead overboard and calling out the depth to the captain on the bridge. Sometimes the steamer gave a great lurch as it struck the bank and became stranded there until the tide turned and refloated her. But not on pantomime day, we hoped.

I recall some simply marvellous pantomimes at Hull, the stories all most faithfully told and embellished with magicians, funny men, demon kings and fairy godmothers and choruses of dancing children. Lavish scenery was always a feature of these shows. Nothing seemed impossible and I remember *Babes in the Wood* with beautiful woodland scenery in which golden leaves fell from the trees and real rabbits hopped about the stage, an effect which produced a long, rapturous 'Aaaaahhh' from the audience.

But everybody's favourite had to be *Cinderella* and as we sat in the theatre waiting for the show to begin the air was electric with anticipation. There was a steady buzz, like several hives of bees, as children took their seats, changed places ('I want to sit next to so-and-so'), took off coats, changed places again ('I can't see') and rattled bags of sweets until the spine-tingling moment arrived when the house lights slowly dimmed. There was a gasp of excitement followed by instant and utter silence as the orchestra struck up a lively tune and the curtain rose to reveal Baron Hardup's kitchen bustling with activity.

Cinderella had all the ingredients with which our romantic hearts

To the pantomime by ferry

could identify and, although we knew perfectly well that she would go to the ball and get her prince in the end, that did not stop us from sharing her disappointments and sorrows – and surprise at the appearance of the Fairy Godmother. The moment we all waited for was the arrival of the coach with those darling white ponies: they really stole the show. There was so much fun; songs to sing that would be with us for days, the brokers' men who smashed huge piles of plates and papered each other to the wall. And the marvellous last scene – all pillars and chandeliers and marble staircases. Maybe there were slight reservations about the principal boy, with her high heels and her strident voice and those soppy love-songs. But the rest was pure heaven and provided us with a whole host of new ideas for our games and play-acting.

Not so amusing was that other from of seasonal entertainment – the children's party. Children's parties were our idea of sheer purgatory. To start with the children were not *our* friends (well, let's face it, we didn't have any): they were the children of our parents' friends and we disliked them all heartily and without exception. The boys were usually rough and used to tease us and pull our hair or knock us over. We had no idea how to stick up for ourselves. The grown-ups used to organize frightful games in which we had to kiss somebody – and they seemed to take an unholy delight in seeing us squirm. Ugh! Can you imagine anything more soppy and embarrassing? But more than anything else we loathed parties because they demonstrated all too clearly our inability to mix with other children and to play with them in a normal way. We felt thoroughly out of our depth and consequently stupid and useless. Pip would spend the first half of the party crying in one corner, while I used the music intended for musical chairs to practise the Charleston (just learnt from my aunt Mint) in another. We really were a dead loss.

The Twelve Days of Christmas drew to a close with an altogether more memorable jollification – a large family supper party that included a great many uncles, aunts and cousins and a few friends. Our young doctor and his wife were both tremendous party-value, being keen members of the local drama club. When it came to games and dressing-up they made such a dynamic contribution to the proceedings that my father was disposed to forgive a telling remark the doctor had once made to him in a light-hearted moment. 'Diagnosis is the thing,' he had said. 'Once you've made up your mind what the patient has got, he'll have it all right!' My father never quite trusted him after that.

For us the party just *had* to be a success because it was the only night of the year we were allowed to stay up late. Besides, we knew everybody and they were all part of our tribe. Truly, blood is thicker than water. Our cousins (seven was the full quota of those available) were all older than Pip and me – Honor's age or even older; some were *really* old and smoked cigarettes in front of their parents so they must have been eighteen, and Cousin Jack arrived sporting an Oxford

University scarf which we found very impressive. But they all entered into the party spirit with great verve and made sure everybody had a good time. The big boy cousins were particulary attentive to us young ones, giving us rides on their shoulders and engaging us in mock battles.

The party started at six o'clock and was preceded by a great rush on the dressing-up chest. My mother had built up a large collection over the years and never let a jumble sale go by without seizing the opportunity to augment it. Granny-bonnets and straw hats, boned bodices and flannel petticoats, together with false noses, beards, masks and tow-hair – the dressing-up chest offered endless possibilities and we children would crowd round, impatiently and plaintively chanting, 'What can I be Mummy? Mummy, what can I be?' She was never short of ideas and would help each one in turn – a pirate with a black eye-patch; a frog with green stockings and large driving-gloves for feet. I always wanted to be something pretty – a flower fairy or a princess. Like my father, I hated being laughed at.

Gradually we would plunder the chest, changing our minds half a dozen times as each garment we retrieved suggested another idea, until we were satisfied and everyone was dressed up. Everyone, that is, except Mummy, who was left behind with the empty chest and a lot of mess to clear up while we swept down the staircase to join the party. A few minutes later Mummy would make her appearance to a great roar of laughter, for out of what was left behind and discarded by the rest of us she had managed to transform herself into a prize-winning entry. On one occasion it was a witch, with green face, blacked-out front teeth, cat, broomstick and all. Another inspiration was a Chinaman in oriental dressing-gown, with a black stocking-top pulled so tightly over her hair that it dragged the corners of her eyes up into appropriately Eastern slits. The stocking hung down the back like a pig-tail and the whole effect was crowned with a large lampshade worn as a hat. But her favourite disguise, in conjunction with her sister Mint, was as one of the Ugly Sisters. They appeared, grotesquely made-up, their tight dresses padded out here and there with balloons, each sister struggling to get through the doorway first. 'Age before beauty, dear!' Mint finally conceded acidly, and got her face slapped. Even the uncles laughed.

When the company was all assembled and the costumes had been

All too soon it was bedtime

admired and prizes given, it was time for supper. The long table in the hall groaned once more with delectable dishes and our shining eyes were bigger than our tummies. Where to start? More to the point, perhaps, when to stop? There were vol-au-vents and game pies, a ham bristling like a hedgehog with cloves, beautiful things in aspic jelly and salads in colourful variety. And the prettiest desserts topped with whipped cream and almonds, cherries and angelica; but the queen of puddings was the trifle. Normally, Cook's trifles were laced liberally with sherry but, as there were certain members of the family who still adhered to the strict Teetotalism of their parents, a special trifle without sherry was made for them. There came a memorable day when George, hovering behind my father's chair, hissed in his ear, 'Sir! sir! Mr Jack has got the *wrong trifle*!' Consternation! But too late. Would our wicked ways be exposed in front of the whole family? But Uncle Jack was beaming and when he opened his mouth it was to say, 'By Jove! This is the best trifle I have ever tasted. Are second helpings permitted?' He seemed unaware of the sigh of relief.

Finally, there was coffee for the grown-ups, cigars for the men and chocolates for everybody and the party began to drift into the drawing-room where, after the briefest interval, we plunged headlong into charades. Biblical themes were favoured because of their strong, well-known stories and because a few sheets, some beards and a halo or two were all that were needed by way of costume and had the added advantage of being quick and easy to change. I have a clear picture of 'Lazarus in Abraham's bosom' in my mind which makes me laugh even now. For these acting games the younger generation was joined by Mint and the doctor and his wife, while the 'oldies' were our audience, sitting by the fire in a cloud of cigar smoke and gossiping quietly during the interminable ages it took us to get our act together. I was reminded of some verses from a favourite poem by William Blake:

Old John with white hair
Doth laugh away care
Sitting under the oak
Among the old folk.

They laugh at our play
And soon they all say

Such, such were our joys
When we all, girls and boys,
In our youthtime were seen
On the Echoing Green.

All too soon someone came to collect Pip and me and whisk us off to bed. But not before we had extracted promises from the cousins to come and say goodnight to us in the nursery. As we trailed reluctantly up the stairs, looking back over our shoulders at the dancing which now began, we were still too elated by the events of the evening to realize how tired we were. Once in bed drowsiness soon began to overtake me and the music and laughter from downstairs seemed to come from another world. Perhaps it wasn't so bad to be a grown-up after all. Grown-ups could do whatever they liked and weren't told they'd make themselves sick or ordered to go to bed at such-and-such a time. When I grow up, I thought, I will eat a whole box of chocolates all by myself, all at once, and stay up dancing *all night*.